UMPHREY LEE
a biography

Winifred T. Weiss & Charles S. Proctor

ABINGDON PRESS
Nashville and New York

UMPHREY LEE: A BIOGRAPHY

Copyright © 1971 by Abingdon Press

ISBN 0-687-42786-X

Library of Congress Catalog Card Number: 76-134245

Quotations from Umphrey Lee, *Our Fathers and Us,* copyright © SMU Press,
1958, are used by permission of Southern Methodist University, Dallas.
Quotations from the *Mustang* magazine, Vol. VI, May 1954, copyright © The
SMU Alumni Association, are used by permission.

SET UP, PRINTED, AND BOUND BY THE
PARTHENON PRESS, AT NASHVILLE,
TENNESSEE, UNITED STATES OF AMERICA

Acknowledgments

Mr. Proctor and I are under obligation to many of Dr. Lee's friends who were generous in granting their time and reminiscences in interviews and letters. Their names appear in the bibliography.

In addition, we are especially grateful to Mrs. John H. Warnick, librarian of the Methodist Collection in the Bridwell Library, Perkins School of Theology, SMU, whose help was invaluable. We wish to thank Dr. Willis M. Tate, president of SMU, and Mrs. Watson A. Tillman, assistant to the President, who made available the files in the Office of the President; Mrs. Edward Beardon and Mr. Ronald C. Knickerbocker of the SMU Archives who assisted us in securing Lee source material. Mr. Eugene McElvaney, chairman of the SMU board of trustees, Dr. Hemphill Hosford, emeritus vice president and provost of SMU, Mrs. Margaret L. Hartley and Mr. Allen Maxwell of the SMU Press read the manuscript and gave assistance and encouragement. Mr. and Mrs. Umphrey Lee, Jr. were interested and cooperative, making available Lee documents and memorabilia in their home.

We are indebted to my husband, Dr. Harold Weiss, for suggesting the rhetorical analysis of Dr. Lee as a notable public speaker which Mr. Proctor presented as his M.A. thesis in the SMU division of Communication Arts; and for later interesting me in developing and expanding the work into a biographical study that became this book. He endured the drudgery of critical reading of our manuscripts and kept us heartened.

Winifred T. Weiss

Dallas, Texas
April 27, 1970

Contents

Preface

Umphrey Lee, scholar, educator, and minister, was one of the most loved and admired Methodist leaders in the South and Southwest. He was an internationally recognized interpreter of John Wesley. Intimately associated with Southern Methodist University through most of his adult life, he was consecutively the pastor of the Highland Park Methodist Church, adjoining the campus; Dean of the School of Religion of Vanderbilt University; President and then Chancellor of SMU. Author of some ten books, uncounted articles, newspaper columns, and a frequent radio commentator, his local reputation was enhanced by a unique ability to preach a twenty-minute sermon or make a fifteen-minute speech that left his delighted audience amused by his gentle wit, uplifted, informed, and enlightened by his penetrating insights.

A versatile, complicated man who exuded an aura of simplicity and unassailable dignity, he captivated those he met informally. In Lady Randolph Churchill's memoirs there is a comparison between Disraeli and Gladstone: "When I left the diningroom after sitting next to Gladstone I thought he was the cleverest man in England. But when I sat next to Disraeli, I felt that I was the cleverest woman." A friend remarked that Umphrey Lee also possessed a genius for making you feel better, bigger, and more intelligent than you really were. He was, perhaps, more interesting even as a personality than as a speaker or writer.

In the last book written by Dr. Lee, *Our Fathers and Us*, these words end the last chapter: "In *Pilgrim's Progress* when

9

Christian had crossed the river and had divested himself of his mortal garments he heard the sound of trumpets and when Mr. Valiant-for-truth passed over 'all the trumpets sounded for him on the other side.' These are great words, among the greatest in our Christian heritage. But I should like most humbly to suggest that the contribution of the Methodists to a changing world was largely in their belief that they on this side of the dark waters caught the sound of trumpets."

Dr. Lee's personality eludes this mound of paper, but those who were fortunate enough to know him as their pastor, their colleague, their college president or friend would agree that he heard the sound of those trumpets; that he epitomized that note of confidence and joyful expectancy that he attributed to Methodism.

I

"I Am Glad I Did Not Close That Door"

Monday, the sixth of November, 1939, was a day that belonged exclusively to Umphrey Lee. On that day he was inaugurated the fourth president of Southern Methodist University. This moment marked the zenith of his career and was a time to be cherished. It was the most important, the most significant day of his life. He would accept no higher position. He had no higher ambition.[1] From that day on there would be no drastic new step. There would be growth and achievement to add luster and distinction to his career, but the progress would be along the line of a plateau with minor ups and downs. His reputation as a speaker would be further enhanced, and he would continue to write. He would gain additional respect and eminence as an educator, and he would continue to be a dominant influence in the North Texas Conference of The Methodist Church for the next fifteen years, but it would be fulfillment and not innovation.

On the morning of his inauguration as president of Southern Methodist University the outlines of Umphrey Lee's life were fully delineated. He had been president of the University's first student body. He had returned twice to teach there, and now

[1] There is agreement among many who knew Dr. Lee that he had no desire to be a bishop, although most say that he could have been had he so wished. They feel that his primary interest was education and that he would not have considered a position the duties of which entailed the shuffling, by appointment, of some 600 ministers a year. He was always hesitant about making a decision by which someone might be hurt. Dr. Lee said, at least once, that he knew he would make a very poor bishop.

11

he was to remain as president and then chancellor for the rest of his life.

Southern Methodist University, its monumental, classically Georgian Dallas Hall, towering in its sea of waving Johnson grass five miles from the heart of Dallas, had enrolled Umphrey Lee and 705 other students in the fall of 1915. This new university, opening its doors for the first time, was the pride of Dallas. Ready to open, the University was presented to Dallas on September 11, 1915. Factory whistles blew and flags waved as the Woodmen of the World Forty-Piece Band, five commands of the Texas National Guard, cars filled with dignitaries, and scores of floats depicting the progress of education from the "Little Red School House," paraded the downtown streets. The celebration ended with a reception and musicale in Dallas Hall. Two thousand citizens made their way by automobile, streetcar, and other assorted means of transportation to consume punch and cookies and tour the new building. It was said, proudly, that 200 cars were parked on the campus during the party.

When registration began on September 22, 1915, Dallas Hall was ready, and four other buildings were in various stages of construction: a Women's Building (now Clements Hall), and three small dormitories for men. (These three burned in 1920.) A small wooden workshop and a structure to house the steam plant were temporary buildings.

But that was 1915 and now, the fall of 1939, Southern Methodist University had begun its twenty-fifth anniversary year. Umphrey Lee was to be inaugurated as president, and both Dallas and SMU had grown and changed. The Johnson grass was gone, and Dallas Hall, commanding an impressive vista down Bishop Boulevard,[2] now dominated a campus of twelve buildings, an athletic stadium, and the partially completed

[2] Named for Dr. Horace Bishop, first chairman of the board of trustees of SMU.

Fondren Library building. The student body had expanded from 706 to 2512 and the teaching staff from thirty-five to almost five times that original number. Dallas, its pioneer vigor in full flower, had increased its population from 125,000 to 290,000 and was rapidly building north, filling in the five miles that had separated central Dallas from the infant university in 1915. Southern Methodist University was still the symbol of the city's cultural progress and its aspirations, and Dallas people had felt actively involved in the selection of SMU's fourth president.

Dallas turned out en masse to welcome Dr. Umphrey Lee on inauguration day. On the campus, McFarlin Auditorium's 2500 seat capacity was not enough and many had to be turned away. Sitting out front that day were prominent Dallas businessmen, members of the SMU board of trustees, friends, ex-students, and University personnel all sharing a vital interest in the future of the University. There was an aura of satisfied euphoria, yet controlled excitement, an assurance that they had the best man to guide the future of the University. The events of inauguration day were a demonstration of mutual trust and affection. There seemed to be a deep satisfaction and a confidence that this man would change the course of the history of SMU and influence all of Dallas.

Ceremonies had begun on Sunday with a religious convocation in the evening in McFarlin Auditorium, Bishop Charles C. Selecman presiding. Bishop Charles L. Mead of Kansas City delivered the sermon.

Monday was one of those perfect days in the extended fall that follows the hot Texas summer. Well before the hour of the formal ceremony visitors began arriving on campus to be sure of securing seats in the auditorium. Soon the faculty began to gather on the steps of Dallas Hall. On a sign from the marshal, Professor Edwin D. Mouzon, Jr., they marched in colorful regalia in academic procession from Dallas Hall to their reserved section in McFarlin Auditorium.

Bishop Ivan Lee Holt presided, and Dr. Oliver C. Carmichael, Chancellor of Vanderbilt University, gave the principal address. Then it was time for the high point of the day. Umphrey Lee rose from his chair at the back of the stage, a big, dignified man with kindly, twinkling eyes behind rimless glasses, and an appealing smile. He wore the long black robe of the Ph.D. degree, and around his neck, flowing down the back, was the hood marked with the light blue and white of Columbia University.

In an impressive traditional ceremony Umphrey Lee accepted the original seal of the University from Bishop A. Frank Smith, chairman of the board of trustees, who said, "Umphrey Lee, I induct you into the presidency of this honored institution with all the rights, honors and obligations attendant to that office." The old friends smiled at each other, and Bishop Smith doffed his mortarboard to the new president.

President Lee's brief inauguration speech was described as having "an almost Gettysburg Address quality." "Dr. Lee, a large man with commanding presence, even more commanding in formal cap and gown, stood before the lectern 'bristling with microphones.' With his eyes glinting with easy good humor, his mellow-timbered voice booming easily through the auditorium, he began his speech, which was interrupted at several points by cheers, . . . from the audience of 2,500 in S.M.U.'s McFarlin Auditorium." [3]

President Lee pointed out that only two institutions, the church and the university, have retained their continuity from the Middle Ages to the present time. He further elaborated on the relationship of the church and university: "No one any longer fears that ownership by a Church will mean narrow sectarianism in the University." He depicted the church and

[3] *Dallas Morning News*, November 7, 1939.

the university as the center of strength of a free nation when he said:

No dictator has been unsophisticated enough to listen to idle chatter about the ineffectiveness of priests and professors. He has known . . . that institutions which claim the right to search for truth in channels other than those prescribed by the state and the freedom to worship a power higher than the state are, with all their faults, the strongholds of a free people.

In the final minutes of the address President Lee expressed a nostalgia for a nobler world and then concluded:

There is a difference between truth and falsehood; there is a difference between kindliness and selfishness. Those who do not in this world learn these things early will profit little by learning anything else.

There was a luncheon for eighty invited guests in Virginia Hall after the ceremony, and inauguration festivities ended with a reception Monday evening in the foyer of Dallas Hall attended by faculty, staff, and hundreds of friends from Dallas and other points. Nine bishops of The Methodist Church, Bishop Charles C. Selecman, Oklahoma City Area; W. C. Martin, Omaha; Ivan Lee Holt, Dallas; A. Frank Smith, Houston; Charles L. Mead, Kansas City; Sam R. Hay, Retired; J. C. Broomfield, St. Louis; Hiram A. Boaz, Retired; J. M. Moore, Retired, had come for the ceremonies as had President Lee's mother, Mrs. Josephus Lee, and J. V. Lee from San Angelo, Texas, Dr. Lee's brother, and his wife.

Dr. Umphrey Lee was young to be a university president, and he was in the full vigor of his forty-six years. Election to the presidency of Southern Methodist University brought into focus his already considerable achievements as a preacher and religious leader, as a writer (six books), an internationally recognized scholar, and an educator. Now he was facing his greatest challenge—the shaping of a university. He would devote himself to a subject ever close to his heart—education.

An impressive number of friends seemed to surround Umphrey Lee at all the important moments of his life. Many were very old friends from youthful days. Almost anybody who knew Umphrey Lee felt that he was a friend and that he knew him well, for his ease of approach and quick perception of people's qualities and frailties were startling and disarming. He produced this phenomenon of rapport seemingly without effort.

Word pictures of this man are always painted in glowing, luminous colors. Most of those who knew him agree that he brought to his new position certain discernible qualities. He was dignified without being pompous; friendly without being effusive; a great scholar, but not lost in an ivory tower; a leader, but not a driver; compassionate, but objective; tolerant, but not permissive; deeply religious without being fanatical or doctrinaire; witty, but gentle. He inspired confidences but did not seek them. He never seemed to hurry but accomplished much. A shining thread of good taste ran through everything he did or said. Always emphasized as the essence of his character is a magnanimous understanding and complete sincerity. All are descriptions that would have embarrassed the modest Lee who always saw his own shortcomings clearly. Superlatives were anathema to a man who was described as "the master of the understatement."

What heritage, what influences, what events shaped the man about whom so many express a sort of gratitude for the privilege of having known him, and who admit that they share in "a universal infatuation with his memory"?

His life spanned a transitional period that moved past the midpoint of the twentieth century. When Umphrey Lee was born in 1893, seven years before the turn of the century, Queen

Victoria was still on the throne of England, the last Czar of the Russians was not yet crowned, and Kaiser Wilhelm's actions had yet to lead to World War I. When Umphrey Lee died at age sixty-five, in 1958, he had lived through two great wars, and the world of the previous century was but a memory. The United States was ten years into the Cold War; the first American troops had been sent to Vietnam; the 1954 Supreme Court decision on civil rights was four years old; and there were stirrings that presaged more violent times to come.

The Lees were variations on the romantic pattern of our idealized pioneers—daring, determined, devout. Umphrey Lee was described by his son as a post-Victorian man, not entirely a modern man; influenced by the aggressive pioneering of his family; but not a captive of the nineteenth century.

Pioneer great-grandfather William Lee was born in Arlington County, Virginia, in the late eighteenth century, possibly a relative of the more famous Lees of Virginia. His marriage to a German immigrant indentured servant girl cut him off from his more snobbish family, and he crossed the Cumberland Gap to make a home near Owensboro, in Barren County (now Daviess County) , Kentucky, as a farmer and shoemaker.

He waded swamp water and lived on raw bacon as a sergeant with Andrew Jackson's forces in the Florida Campaign of the War of 1812, and his son, Isaac B. Lee, came home from the Mexican War in 1848 with a wound that left him with a pronounced limp.

Isaac boldly took the minority side in Kentucky during the Civil War and, when the Confederates put a price on his head, he left all he owned and fled to safer territory in Indiana with only two horses, a wagon, his wife, and his eight children to start life anew when he was past middle age. Umphrey Lee was impressed by his grandfather Isaac and later wrote: "There was something awe-inspiring about beards, particularly to young children. My own grandfather was a deacon in the church and,

17

I know now, a kind father; but I was scared to death of him. He wore a long beard that probably concealed the lack of a necktie. When I knew him he had reached the ripe old age of 60. But to me he was as old as Moses and as impressive." ("As I See It," June 2, 1957.)

Isaac's son, Josephus Lee, was ordained as minister in the General Baptist Church in 1879. He lived to a venerable age and was married three times. His first wife died soon after marriage, but the second wife lived to give him two sons, Luther and Vaden. The wife of his middle and late years, and the mother of Umphrey, was Mrs. Esther Davis Harris, a widow whose husband and two of her small daughters were killed in a destructive cyclone that struck the Delaware community in McLean County, Kentucky, on March 27, 1890. Mrs. Harris was severely injured and during her long recuperation a local pastor and circuit rider, widower Josephus Lee, was a frequent visitor. They were married in 1892 and moved to Oakland City, Indiana. Umphrey Lee was born there on March 23 of the next year.

Soon the family moved on to other pastorates, and Umphrey attended high school in Missouri. Preachers in those days were frequently men of limited education, preaching to a flock of similar meager learning. Sermons tended to be evangelistic and, in a short time, both the preacher and his congregation were worn out with each other. Preachers were usually moved after one or two years. Self-educated Josephus Lee was an exception, but his intense, bombastic temperament did not correlate with long tenure.

Grandfather Isaac Lee was the first preacher in the family, and Josephus followed him into the church whose teachings and doctrines greatly influenced his son, Umphrey Lee. The General Baptist Church, following the Arminian tradition of open or general communion, was organized in England in 1611. King James I proclaimed them heretics, along with other

18

religious protest groups, and by proclamation commanded that they leave England. Many fled to America where they were formally organized by Roger Williams.

During the next hundred years the General Baptists followed the westward migration. Many settled in Kentucky and later in Indiana, Missouri, and Illinois. These states seem to have formed a regular circuit for the itinerant pioneer preachers.

The nineteenth century was not a placid time in these pioneer states, and the General Baptists did not preach a placid religion. Both Isaac and his son Josephus were fighters espousing a faith that refused to take second place in the lives of converts. Isaac and his gun-toting congregation one time subdued a terrorist Ku Klux Klan group that marched into the service, rope in hand, all set to hang the preacher. Josephus Lee was an undismayed champion of Populism who ran for congress in Missouri on the Populist ticket, missed election by a narrow margin, and continued for a time to edit a Populist newspaper for which Umphrey set type as a small boy.

The young Umphrey had firsthand knowledge of America's heritage of violence. The 1890's and early 1900's were marked by a deep feeling of unrest and frustration that erupted into desperation and outrage. The agricultural midwest suffered increasing maladjustments. Good cheap farming land had been absorbed, freight rates were increasingly high, tenant farmers and small independent debtor farmers felt the squeeze of high interest rates and lowered income. There were desperation demands for cheap money, a more flexible banking system, lower tariffs, and an end to trusts and monopolies. Traditional party loyalties weakened and led to the organization of a party of revolt, the Populists. Many lost confidence in direct political action and feeling ran high. Politics, religion, and the economic situation became hopelessly confused. Hysteria led to violence. After the Civil War, Republican majorities were the rule in

19

much of the midwest, and in some areas Populists were considered worse than Democrats.

Newell Sims in his published doctorate dissertation, *A Hoosier Village,* recounted the incident of a respected member of the town election board who was removed from the board and "shunned by his comrades" for allowing an occupant of his house to display a Bryan picture from a window.

As a boy of twelve, Umphrey and his father had the experience of being barricaded in the home of a fellow Populist under attack from night riders who had earlier planted a sign, "Prepare to meet thy God," in the front yard. The host and Umphrey's father were armed with guns while Umphrey was given a butcher knife and stationed by an unlikely window prepared to stab if anyone tried to enter. He was taut with excitement as he saw shadowy figures of men dodging in and out of the bushes. A few shots were fired, apparently enough to be convincing, for the attackers gave up and went away.

Josephus actively supported William Jennings Bryan. Eventually, in 1908, Umphrey was old enough to share his father's campaigning for Bryan. By this time Umphrey had quite a local reputation as a high school debater and was dubbed, "The Boy Orator of Missouri," in proud imitation of Bryan, "The Boy Orator of the Platte." Umphrey appeared for a time on the Chatauqua platform as "The Boy Orator." When the Lee family moved to Texas a friend reported that sixteen-year-old Umphrey was visibly embarrassed by his father's introducing him everywhere as "The Boy Orator" while flourishing laudatory newspaper clippings about him.

Umphrey Lee, no doubt, remembered his youth and the William Jennings Bryan campaign when he wrote later of old-fashioned political oratory:

And all the purple passages were really purple. Senator Ollie James of Kentucky is supposed to have risen indignantly when a bill was introduced to buy cavalry horses in Wyoming. "You might as well," roared the senator, "talk about sending a cordon of angels from the pearly parapets of paradise to the region of the damned to look for good society as to send anywhere but to Kentucky for saddle horses." I did not hear the senator, but I know he waved his hands; he had to when he referred to "the pearly parapets of paradise." ("As I See It," December 30, 1956.)

Josephus Lee had a great influence upon his son, and Umphrey returned admiration and affection. Umphrey Lee's religious convictions, his inquiring mind, his interest in contemporary life, all bore the imprint of Josephus Lee. There was deep understanding between Umphrey Lee and his father. Although unlike each other in personality, there was mutual acceptance and appreciation. One time, while Umphrey was a student at SMU, Harrison Baker, a student friend, went with Umphrey to the railroad station to see the elder Lee off on a trip. As usual, Umphrey kissed his father good-bye. A man standing close by said to Umphrey, "Is that your dad?" And when Umphrey answered, "Yes," the man said, "Shake," and extended his hand.

A picture of Josephus Lee taken about 1916 shows a strong resemblance to his son in his later years if you visualize the father's face without the bushy Grover Cleveland-type mustache. There are the same hairline, nose, full round chin, short neck, and direct kindly gaze.

But in many ways they were not alike. Not only a difference in temperament but, possibly, the observation of cause and effect in the tumultuous life of the elder Lee led Umphrey to avoid the "head-on," "full-battle-cry" approach to problems. Logic and persuasion were substituted for the father's ebullience of emotion.

Josephus Lee was a large man, near 300 pounds at one time, with deep convictions and a fierce fighting temperament, proud, acutely sensitive, and animated by a driving energy. He preached, he conducted revival meetings, he sold life insurance, he edited and published *The General Baptist,* he was active in politics, he ran his farm, and he was a good husband and father to his three sons and one stepdaughter, as attested to by the long devotion of his wife and his children. Umphrey Lee dedicated two of his books to his father.

Turn-of-the-century congregations did not support their preachers in luxury. Umphrey Lee remarked once, when asked if he would accept a box of cigars for a Christmas present, that he could hardly be against tobacco when his father as a preacher in Kentucky was often paid in tobacco. Josephus Lee was looked up to as a knowledgeable person but, as his son said, "He had no formal education and the elements of learning were worked out before a fireplace full of pine knots." ("The Clouds Return After the Rain.") The elder Lee held learning in high regard, and young Umphrey was no disappointment to his father. He was a bright, intelligent child who absorbed knowledge like a sponge.

In the tradition of frequent pastorate changes, the Lees moved often. Sometimes the family home was several miles from the school, and Umphrey walked, rain, shine, or snow. These small, midwestern schools at the turn of the century were usually one-room affairs containing one teacher for all grades and subjects, one pot-bellied stove, a blackboard and perhaps a few maps on pull-down rollers. The library, whether public school or private college, consisted mainly of a copy of Horace's Odes and a Latin grammar. The textbooks were probably Noah Webster's "blue-backed" *American Spelling Book* and McGuffey's *Reader.*

The omnipresent art work carved on the desk tops was mute testimony to the fact that most of the students lacked profound interest in scholarly pursuits or in the Psalms, aphorisms, and religious information contained in the McGuffey and Webster textbooks. Nevertheless, the reluctant student learned to decode "Cider is made from apples," along with "God created the heavens and the earth in six days, and all that was made was good." Discipline was usually a problem with the harried teacher and, no doubt, a "low-achiever" struggling to decipher "I will kiss the babe on his cheek," followed by the admonition "Shut the gate to keep out the hogs," contributed to the problem.

Umphrey did not make an outstanding record in elementary school, but his high school record was all A's as was his college record. He was an omnivorous reader, an active high school debater and orator, but he still found plenty of time for sports and athletics. In high school he was a high jumper and sprinted the 100-yard dash. For a time he thought of continuing as an amateur athlete but gave this up in college.

Umphrey Lee was still being identified as an athlete when he entered Southern Methodist University in 1915, although his interest in competition had waned some time before. For a few years he continued to play tennis. Many years later he said that if an archaeologist, hundreds of years in the future, dug into a ruin which had once been Lee's home, he would probably conclude that a prominent sportsman had lived there, the house would be so well equipped with an array of sports equipment—fishing tackle, shotguns, tennis rackets, and golf clubs. He had once enjoyed all these sports, as well as camping, riding, and volley ball. The excavators would never suspect that only the fishing and hunting gear were significant artifacts.

Josephus Lee survived many stormy pastorates, but the General Baptists did not tolerate an independent thinker and theological dissenter indefinitely. He "ventured to express some doubts concerning the doctrine of infant damnation. He was tried for heresy and expelled from communion." [4] Supple-

---

[4] Walter N. Vernon, *Methodism Moves Across North Texas.*

mentary charges were that he was an anti-footwasher, cried in excess of emotion, and was undermining the church by pretending that a movement was on to unite the Free and General Baptists. So he entered politics and joined the Methodist Church. The first shock at the action of the church to which he had devoted his life had hardly worn off when Josephus had the first attack of the asthma that plagued him for several years. His doctor, conveniently, recommended that he should move, perhaps to a warmer climate.

Umphrey was sixteen when the Lees boarded the train for the long trip to Texas in 1909. They arrived in Waco at night, and as they drove by buggy through the moonlight into the country to their destination, Mrs. Lee was cheered to see the forms of beautiful orchards and fields stretching out across the flat land. With the daylight the fruit trees turned into mesquite bushes on a dry, arid plain.

The same year Josephus requested the Northwest Texas Conference of the Methodist Episcopal Church, South for an appointment as minister. His fifty-eight years was considered too old and he was rejected, but, reconsidering, the conference sent him to the small town of Zephyr, Texas, in the Brownwood district.

Thirty years later when Josephus Lee was dead and Umphrey Lee had become president of Southern Methodist University, he was asked to preach at a meeting of the Sulphur Springs District Conference of the Methodist Church, meeting in Cumby, Texas. His text was, "Behold, I have set before you an open door," and his theme was, "The church is the opener of doors." After his sermon, Dr. J. Sam Barcus, the district superintendent, said, "A few years ago I was chairman of admissions for the Central Texas Conference and a man asked to be admitted. He was a Baptist and he said to the committee that he was fifty-eight years old and would not be worth much to the Methodist Church, but, 'I have a son, Umphrey, who will

24

ask for admittance if I am received.' " Dr. Barcus then added, "I am glad I did not close that door."

The next year, 1910, the Rev. James H. Stewart, Sr., presiding elder of the Brownwood district, took seventeen-year-old Umphrey into his home, and he was enrolled as a Freshman in Daniel Baker College. He was a shy, retiring but brilliant student. However, he gained confidence, joined the debate squad, engaged in amateur parlor theatricals, continued his interest in athletics, and began his preaching career in the nearby country churches.

Umphrey was soon on the staff of the *Daniel Baker Collegian* as an exchange editor. The *Collegian* was published monthly by the Delta Kappa Sigma, Pi Alpha, and McClelland Literary societies, and Umphrey made the most of his opportunity as a contributor. In the March 1911 issue he declared that the "first object of the exchange department is to give readers the cream of other college publications. The second reason—a very important one—is to give useful criticism," which he proceeded to do for four of the magazine's twenty-five pages. He objected to a parody on the twenty-third Psalm in one of the exchanges. He felt that it was not necessary to "resort to the scriptures for amusement."

The next year he was editor-in-chief of the college paper, *The Trail*. Umphrey was happy at Daniel Baker but, presumably, Josephus found it difficult to finance board and room plus other college expenses, and it was decided that Umphrey should make a change. On stationery of *The Trail* Umphrey wrote on December 1, 1912, to Miss Mary Sweet that he would go home to Red Oak at Christmas and commute from there to Trinity University in Waxahachie on the interurban. He found it hard to say good-bye to Brownwood, "the only place I have really stayed in Texas. . . . No more tramping over these hills and no more pulling through the sand. But I refrain from anymore such tearful comments. Henceforth *at home* daily."

At this point he was interrupted by a Miss Gertrude who brought him some divinity on the point of a butcher knife and he ended his letter, "At least I'm temporarily resigned to
> Lethe's dreamless ooze
> The common grave (the unventurous throng) .
Well, well, what is to be will be."

(Mary Sweet, who taught English for forty-two years at North Texas State, Denton, Texas, was a childhood friend of Umphrey Lee. The Sweet and Lee families were friends in Brownwood, Texas. Both children attended Daniel Baker College. Nine letters written by Umphrey Lee to Mary Sweet from December 1, 1912, to November 10, 1916, were saved by Miss Sweet and after her death were kept by her niece, Mrs. Tom Beaty. They are now in the archives at Southern Methodist University.)

At Trinity University in Waxahachie, Umphrey was soon living again at the home of the presiding elder of the Waxahachie district, the Rev. John Whitehurst, and paid the five-cent fare to ride to Trinity each day on the streetcar. The Rev. Whitehurst had helped the Lees get settled in Texas and Josephus Lee assigned to a pastorate. Word soon got around that a very bright boy was living in the Whitehurst home, and that the boy was also a fine debater. Ilion T. Jones, who later became a well-known Presbyterian scholar and writer, was considered the champion debater in that area of Texas. A debate with this untried quantity, Umphrey Lee, was arranged. The debate subject was "independence of the Philippines," with Jones in the affirmative and Lee in the negative.

In 1914, a college debate was a big event in Waxahachie. Townspeople packed the auditorium—there was even a "sprinkling of local lawyers." Lee's "matchless oratory" was a surprise to the audience as well as to Jones. However, eloquence was not the determining factor, and Umphrey won on a technicality. The wording of the proposition read: "Resolved that the Philippines should be granted their independence in fifteen years as Congress may by law prescribe." Jones, the affirmative speaker, outlined an elaborate plan of education to prepare the citizens of the Philippines for self-government. Lee, the negative speaker, elaborately orated his agreement with Jones and commented to the effect that the educational plan had great merit but it was impossible to debate the subject because the wording of the proposition "overlooked the fact that no one could predict what Congress would do, especially in fifteen years!" Humor, logically related to his premise, would win many battles for Lee in the years to come, but, although in debate his asides sometimes scorched severely, they never really burned, for he was simply "a real gentleman."

After that triumph Umphrey went on to win a gold medal as proof of his debating prowess. While attending Trinity, he coached the local high school debate team. Two young and eager members of the team were Albert Sydney Johnson and Hastings Harrison. Lee coached the youths to a trophy as champions of Ellis County. Many years later, General Johnson, an outstanding lawyer as well as general, made the statement that he had learned his first law from Umphrey when he was corrected on his pronunciation of "indictment."

Umphrey's perfect scholastic record continued, and he received his A.B. degree from Trinity in 1914. That same year he was ordained a deacon in the Methodist Church, South, and the Rev. Whitehurst assigned him to fill the pulpit at the First Methodist Church in Ennis, Texas. As a young guest speaker, he had "electrified" the congregation, and they had petitioned the bishop to let Lee fill out the conference year although he was far too young for such a post.

He was in Ennis full-time during the long hot summer. He complained about the mosquitoes in his little study but postponed any protective action until the next summer—if he stayed on! He visited the sick. In March he had reached his twenty-first birthday, and in the fall he went home to Ferris to cast his first vote. He was introduced to the game of volley ball and had some sore muscles. He played tennis and was invited out to dinner by various parishioners. He entertained his brother who came to visit and apparently overstayed his welcome. At least, Umphrey noted in one letter to Mary Sweet that his brother "is still here and shows no signs of going home."

He worked hard on his sermons and prepared some lectures on "Paul" for the YMCA. He had money worries, and on August 27 he wrote, "If my stewards do not see me directly, I shall have to hunt up my old checkbook, and go to drawing on papa, as is my custom in emergencies—and other times."

Umphrey Lee's future was already taking a discernible shape. He was fortunate in an environment where he early discovered the power of words and the excitement of books. English was "the old standby" to him, not courses in education. He did much dreaming over his future. The quarterly conference was only two months off, and what would that mean to him? Should he plan to go on to graduate school? He would like to go to Princeton and then, "when the war cools down," on to Heidelberg or Oxford. He thought he definitely would try for a Ph.D. "It's one of papa's dearest wishes, and I hope to satisfy it."

The letter to Mary Sweet on August 20, 1914, refers to World War I. On June 28, 1914, Archduke Franz Ferdinand, heir to the throne of Austria-Hungary, was assassinated at Sarajevo in the province of Bosnia, and soon the war began that had been threatening Europe since the beginning of the century. Serbia, blamed for the assassination, refused to concede to all of Austria's stringent demands, and on July 28, Austria declared war on her. In quick succession, Germany declared war on Russia and France, Great Britain declared war on Germany, and all the great European powers were involved.

"I Am Glad I Did Not Close That Door"

In 1914, the average American did not realize that the war in Europe would affect him directly and vitally. There was an almost universal sentiment of isolationism and a determination to stay out of any foreign conflict. Umphrey Lee was already interested in history and later became a close student of world affairs, but at age 21 in Ennis, Texas, he was still a provincial young man, absorbed in his own affairs and detached from the momentous happenings of the time. Other letters from this period do not mention the war.

The church at Ennis and revival meetings in other Texas towns occupied the young man all that year. He preached in Waco, Bruceville, Mt. Calvin, Dublin, and other small towns. He thought he should lose some of his 165 pounds, and he was eager to get on to graduate school, someplace. He considered Harvard University. During the summer he wrote that he had read two books in Greek and Pope's translation of the *Iliad*.

"He was also attracted by the Idea as an entity, a heritage from his early life as a minister's boy in a home that was no stranger to philosophy" [5] and, after studying the Harvard and Southern Methodist University catalogues, he decided that he wanted to study the Philosophy of the Christian religion. In the end, he made a trip to Dallas on the interurban to talk to the professors of the new Southern Methodist University to be opened in September with a graduate department in Theology that would offer a Master's degree. And so began Umphrey Lee's long association with Southern Methodist University.

[5] Paul Crume, "SMU Honors First Student President, Now Head of School."

II

"Where the Saints Are"—1915-1923

Graduate student Umphrey Lee, age 22, did not arrive unheralded on the Southern Methodist University campus. The hastily organized *SMU Times* noted that one Umphrey Lee from Ferris, Texas, had arrived to enroll for study toward the Master's degree and added that, "Mr. Lee is known quite widely in the state as an inter-collegiate debater and also as an athlete." Probably Umphrey came from Ferris on the interurban, took the streetcar on Elm Street in downtown Dallas, as arriving resident students were instructed to do, and transferred to the tiny streetcar, appropriately nicknamed the "Dinky," for the remainder of the five-mile trip to the campus. Later Lee spoke of the tendency of the "Dinky" to get off the track when it tried to round the last curve to the campus, and of the passengers' participation in getting it back on to complete the run.[1]

John Whitehurst, Umphrey Lee's roommate at Trinity, had the job of showing new students to their rooms in the new dorms. "Actually," he said, "they just picked their rooms, for the walls were not yet finished at registration time." Prices ranged from $6 to $12 per month for rooms, depending upon size, number of occupants, and luxury of appointments, and table board was $16 per month. Part of the year, at least, Umphrey did not live in the dormitory but got up very early to ride the interurban each day from Ferris to Dallas.

The young Umphrey Lee who lined up for registration on

[1] Many years later a gilded spike from the "Dinky" tracks, preserved by Stanley Patterson, was presented to Dr. Lee.

September 22, 1915, was easily distinguishable. He was a large young man, over six feet, dignified, eyes smiling through his glasses, and he always wore the highest, stiffest starched white collars on the campus around his size 17½ neck.

After registration, the first of the compulsory chapels was presided over by Dr. R. S. Hyer, first president of the fledgling institution. He apparently had heard of the young preacher Umphrey Lee but did not know him. After a few welcoming remarks, he called on student W. Harrison Baker to lead the student body in fifteen "rahs" for SMU. Then Dr. Hyer announced that he was going to call on both a student and a member of the faculty for a few words.

Looking at the front row of seats in the Dallas Hall Chapel, he said, "I want Umphrey Lee to represent the student body." All was silence for a few seconds, and no one moved until Dr. Hyer pointed at student Ed Tidwell and said, "I mean you." Ed Tidwell, much flustered and embarrassed, finally blurted out, "I am not Umphrey Lee." Umphrey Lee had missed the first compulsory chapel but, from then on, his name was well known on campus.

Two weeks later, on October 5, a student mass meeting began the process of campus organization. Umphrey Lee was temporary chairman and one of a committee of eight to supervise the election of student officers. On October 9, 400 of the 706 students voted.[2] Umphrey Lee was elected president of the student body; Robert W. Goodloe, president of the students in the graduate school; W. Harrison Baker, editor of the student paper which he hastened to rename *The SMU Campus* in the second quarter. The three became leaders in Texas Methodism and devoted friends. Lee and his Executive Committee had the opportunity to inaugurate activities and develop campus spirit and attitudes unfettered by tradition.

During the first quarter they assisted in initiating the honor

[2] 590 of the 706 were full-time students the first quarter (Hosford).

system on the campus and made a deep impression on the undergraduates. Among other things the Executive Committee launched intramurals and organized several girls' basketball teams; set up dormitory rules; named the athletic team; started intercollegiate debating; planned the first annual, *The Rotunda*; levied a twenty-five-cent poll tax to finance the Student Association; and tackled the problem of beautifying the grounds. Scores of letters went to families and friends asking for donations of trees, shrubs, and flowers. At first they were not able to do much about replacing the Johnson grass or getting enough real sidewalks where boards were laid across the mud, and it was several years before the hog lot was gone from its location near the power plant. But that year the sixty or more hogs fed from table scraps returned to the tables as pork or were profitably sold to finance purchases of other food.

Umphrey Lee always maintained that his election as president of the first student body was an accident. Since most of the students were transfers from old Polytechnic in Fort Worth or Southwestern in Georgetown, they paired off trying to pick a president. "I had come from Trinity, so they settled on me as a last choice," he said. In 1915, Dallas Hall, the lone classroom-administration building, was built around a rotunda that extended up all three stories. It was also the foyer, and access to all classrooms and offices was through this circular room. A friend, who was also a student at SMU that year, liked to maintain, humorously, that Umphrey was elected student body president because he stood around in the rotunda several times a day. Everyone passing through saw him, and he looked so much like a president that they elected him.

All year Umphrey Lee was a whirlwind of activity. He helped organize the first fraternity on campus, Delta Sigma Phi. He was one of the student assistant-superintendents of the Sunday school organized in the chapel on the third floor of Dallas Hall. In November he spoke to the campus YMCA on "The

Schedule of Time." Among other speaking engagements was a Lyceum lecture to the students of Meridian College and two sermons at the First Methodist Church in Dublin, Texas.

In addition, he was busy helping his father raise funds for the Methodist Orphanage at Waco. He missed a week of school in February while on the lecture platform.

In April, the school paper had a headline, "Where the Saints Are," commenting in a chatty tone, "Reverend Umphrey Lee . . . called upon by directors of the Bardwell Public School to preach the Commencement sermon. . . . A little bird whispers that this is Umphrey's wise way of rounding up stray greenbacks. We are informed, also, that the Reverend U. Lee will begin a two-weeks' revival in St. John's Methodist Church, Dallas, next week. Best Wishes."[3]

Umphrey's name did not appear often in the social column of the *Campus*. He was not present at an early taffy pull given by Miss Julia Mouzon, daughter of Bishop Edwin D. Mouzon, for senior and graduate students, but his name is listed as a guest of the same Miss Mouzon and her sister at a later date. Presumably Umphrey performed well when it became his turn to act out the title of a book, but he did not win first prize and so lost his chance to own "a beautiful leather-bound volume of Havergal's poems." His friends Goodloe, Baker, eleven other young men, and seventeen girls made up the rest of the party group that evening.

The first issue of the Southern Methodist University yearbook, *The Rotunda*, published in the spring of 1916, included eight full pages of college-type humor, and Umphrey Lee was not overlooked. He was tabbed, "Printer's Devil," in the pseudo staff listings, but in the comic stories his name was more often linked with the faculty than with the students.

John Whitehurst was probably Umphrey's closest friend on

³ *SMU Campus*, April 8, 1916.

the campus. Sometime during the year they were invited back
to Brownwood for a class reunion. A friend told them that the
banquet was to be formal. They succeeded in attiring themselves in tuxedos and presented themselves at the gala affair.
Someone had given them the wrong information. Only
Umphrey, John Whitehurst, and the head waiter at the hotel
were so splendidly dressed.

Mr. Frank Seay, Professor of New Testament in the School
of Theology at Southern Methodist University, was one of the
important influences in Umphrey Lee's life. He was not only
an inspiration for a young man who was in need of guidance
and assurance but he gave Lee a strong foundation in scholarship. When Umphrey Lee arrived at Columbia University and
Union Theological Seminary in New York to begin work toward the Ph.D. degree in the fall of 1916, the University was
doubtful about admitting a graduate of unknown, one-year-
old Southern Methodist University in far-off Dallas. Some sort
of oral examination to evaluate his preparation was decreed.
Umphrey was apprehensive, but not for long. It soon became
apparent that Professor Seay had tutored him well. Umphrey
had read the right books, and he was soon at ease with the
questioners who were, in turn, impressed by the knowledge
and intelligence of the prospective student.

The Lee family was proud when SMU conferred its first
seven Master's degrees in the spring of 1916 and Umphrey
stepped up to receive his diploma. In September he set out
for New York and his first heady contact with the big city.
Maurice T. Moore, a Trinity friend and former debating
partner, was his roommate when he enrolled at Columbia
University and Union Theological Seminary. In November
there was the spectacle of New York through two days and
nights of excited uncertainty over the outcome of the presidential election. In early returns Charles Evans Hughes surged
ahead with the Eastern vote and was thought to have won. The

next day, when the Western vote began to come in, Woodrow Wilson, on his slogan of "He Kept Us Out of War," received his electoral majority. Umphrey stayed up late both suspenseful nights enthralled by the excitement in the city.

By this time Umphrey had decided to major in philosophy, specializing in the Hellenistic period. He was hard at work on German, Greek, and Latin, and busy as director of religious education at the Church of the Holy Apostle. New York was an exciting experience for the small-town boy who had "always been inclined to be rather Puritanical," and there were many trips to the economical "family circle" at the Metropolitan Opera House. The theater intrigued him, and he saw John Drew in "Major Tendencies," David Warfield in "The Music Master," "Century Girl," and "Turn to the Right" at the Gaiety. Yet references to opera, music, art, or the theater are strangely missing from Umphrey Lee's speaking or writings that are so liberally sprinkled with references to the classics and current literature.

His greatest thrill was to hear Benjamin Jowett, the famous Greek scholar and "mighty master" of Balliol at Oxford who had molded so many of the ruling class of England, and to study under Professors Tryon, Franklin Henry Giddings, James Harvey Robinson, and John Dewey.

Umphrey Lee was particularly fortunate in his college and university professors or, perhaps, he was the student that teachers dream about—a young man with a high quality of intelligence, an eager curious mind, and sufficiently un-sophisticated to stimulate the teacher's best efforts. There had been Professor Livingston, professor of English at Trinity University, and Professor Seay at Southern Methodist University. After that there was a professor at Columbia in 1916 whom Lee remembered but did not name. He maintained, in retrospect:

I remember men more than I do subjects. And when I ask why I have been interested for these decades, . . . I realize it was certain men. . . . I remember the professor, in New York of all places, who took me through flower gardens and through the Metropolitan Museum, showing me Paul Revere's silverware and glass by people I never heard of and haven't remembered, trying to teach an ignorant boy that there are more things in the world than can be confined between the covers of a book.[4]

In November, Umphrey was writing that he hoped to spend the summer and the next winter in New York working toward that coveted Ph.D., but by spring, Columbia was "almost completely broken up by the war." (The United States had declared war on the central powers on April 6, 1917.) In May, Umphrey was back at SMU teaching classes in "Ethics" and "Present Tendencies in Philosophy" to release Dean John H. Keen to join wartime secret service in Washington, D.C. Columbia had allowed Lee to take his final examinations early so that no credit was lost.

The year 1917 was a crisis year for the world and a major turning point for Umphrey Lee. Intensely patriotic and passionately attached to the cause of freedom and justice, he felt that he must serve in some way. A return to Columbia was out of the question and the army refused his services when he tried to enlist. Few people ever realized that Umphrey Lee was almost totally blind in one eye and suffered some sort of muscular imbalance that became more noticeable in later years, particularly under a stress situation. The opportunity to help came when the Central Texas Annual Conference of the Methodist Church, South accepted him as an undergraduate, admitted him on trial, and appointed him missionary to Aviation Camps one and three in Texas.

With the Ph.D. dream postponed and his establishment as

---

[4] President's report to the board of trustees of Southern Methodist University, November 12, 1952.

a full-fledged minister, Umphrey reached a decision on another vital question. He decided to marry. He had met Mary Margaret Williams when he was a member of the Daniel Baker College debate team. One trip took the squad to Southwestern University in Georgetown, Texas. His friend, A. Frank Smith, later Bishop Smith, arranged there a double date to include Umphrey. He did not forget the attractive girl he met on this blind date. She had completed two years at Southwestern University and then transferred to the University of Texas to complete her A.B. Degree.

Miss Mary Margaret Willaims and the Rev. Umphrey Lee were married at Christmastime in 1917. The new Mrs. Lee was born in Gatesville, Texas, the daughter of a well-to-do merchant and cattleman. Her marriage to Umphrey Lee was opposed by Josephus and Esther Lee, possibly because of the vast differences in backgrounds of the two young people. The Williams family was not religious or "church going," and seemed to have an attitude that ignored the seriousness of the Lees and their attitude toward life. There remained a coolness and formality between Mary and Esther Lee that was never bridged.

Mary Lee recognized that she had not been brought up to be a minister's wife and felt this keenly, but she was eager to learn and do all that she could to help her husband. Her participation in women's groups was particularly frightening to her, and Umphrey was called upon to write out her little speeches, devotionals, and prayers for her to memorize until she became more experienced and confident.

Newly ordained as an elder at the November 1918 conference in Mineral Wells, Texas, the Rev. Umphrey Lee was appointed to the Cisco Station in Cisco, Texas, and went to work with his usual energy. Before the year was over arrangements were completed for the construction of a new $50,000 church building in Cisco. The *Journal* of the conference lists the salary of the minister at Cisco that year as the princely sum of $2000 per annum.

After only a year at the Cisco pastorate Lee could not resist the lure of the academic world when he was offered the director-ship of the Wesley Bible Chair at the University of Texas. The North Texas Conference had voted to allocate $600 supple-mentary support for the chair, making the post more attractive, but Umphrey Lee's predilection for scholarship and teaching were deciding factors. In Austin he chanced to find some of the documents that furnished the basic material for his Ph.D. thesis and at least four of his books.

Major George W. Littlefield, a successful Texas cattle baron, had been persuaded to purchase the Wrenn collection of eighteenth-century English books, pamphlets, newspapers, etc. for the University of Texas. The Lees met the curator of the Wrenn collection while house-hunting. They tactfully declined to rent curator R. H. Griffith's house for the summer when inspection showed that it was little more than "four walls and a Pope library." But Professor Griffith put Lee to work on some tedious research details for him, and Umphrey Lee discovered that this was to be his most satisfying metier—research into the life and work of John Wesley.

Book catalogues, particularly rare book catalogues, were the "wish books" of the budding young scholar, Umphrey Lee, whose ministerial salary could not support many extravagant purchases. But, for the Wesley Bible Chair at the University of Texas, there were unused library funds. During Lee's two years in Austin, the library accumulated a valuable collection of Wesley material. In his selections he showed great biblio-graphic foresight. This was the beginning of his long search for primary sources dealing with the early years of Methodism.

The rare Wesley collection was purchased at a total cost of $1,250. Today, more than fifty years later, the collection is almost priceless. All materials are by or about John and Charles

Wesley and the history of Methodism. In the collection are 101 items published during John Wesley's lifetime, twenty-one of them are first editions, several as early as the 1740's. There are 126 books on the history of Methodism, and the remaining are works by or about persons in England during and following Wesley's time. There are first editions of Wesley's *Hymns* and treatises dealing with the doctrines of election and reprobation, predestination, and the principles of Methodism, as well as *Thoughts on Marriage and the Single Life,* all published in the 1740's. One of the most valuable items is a copy of *Life of Our Blessed Lord and Savior* by Samuel Wesley, the father of John Wesley, a first edition, published in 1693. (A later 1697 edition of the work was listed at $150 several years ago.)

A few years ago, the Wesley collection was purchased from the University of Texas and is now in the Bridwell Library at Southern Methodist University.

Umphrey Lee soon began writing for publication. In 1921, an article by him appeared in the *Proceedings of the Wesley Historical Society* (England), entitled "America. Lewis Timothy, Charlestown. The Printer of Wesley's First Hymn Book, 1737," a story about the connection of this early printer with the Wesleys who arrived in America February 28, 1735.

A 1924 issue of the *Proceedings* refers to a communication from Umphrey Lee, written earlier in Ennis, Texas, about research relative to a famous attempt by the French prophets to raise from the dead a "Dr." Emes, thought to be the case referred to by Wesley in one of his sermons.

Home for the Lees in Austin became the lower unit of an apartment complex. Umphrey was up early each morning for a game of tennis at 6 A.M. with a young man whose upstairs apartment overlooked the Lees' terrace. One fine morning in late spring the tennis game had to be postponed until a measure of peace descended on the Lee household. The neighbors,

Dallas and Loretta Hawkins, breakfasted to the sound of angry accusations and counter-accusations from the Lee terrace. It appeared that pretty Mary Lee had collected rain water to wash her brown hair. Umphrey Lee had been reading and had left a stack of books on the terrace. The rain water had been spilled; some of the water had dampened the books. Mary Lee was upset because her precious soft water had been lost; Umphrey Lee was furious because his precious books had been damaged.

After two years at the University of Texas, Umphrey Lee took Mary with him to New York for more work toward the Ph.D. degree at Columbia. Then the Lees were back in Ennis, Texas, where Umphrey had been first appointed as minister while a student at Trinity University. This time the stipend was $3,000. One more successful year passed and, in 1923, the Rev. Umphrey Lee transferred to the North Texas Conference and began his thirteen-year tenure at the Highland Park Methodist Church in Dallas, Texas.

Like his father and grandfather before him, Umphrey Lee had his own, though somewhat different, confrontation with one of the extra-legal terrorist groups. While serving at one of his small-town pastorates in Texas, word came to him that the Ku Klux Klan, in full regalia, planned the next Sunday to march into the church and up to the pulpit to present a sizable gift of money to the church. Lee hunted up one of the local businessmen who was a great joiner and asked him to convey the message to the Klan that if this happened he would resign *on the spot*. Nothing happened and nothing more was said. A year or two later, after he had left that pastorate, Lee made an inquiry about who in his congregation was a member of the Klan. He was told that *all* members of his official board had been members. A lengthy meeting had been held about his ultimatum, and only by a close decision was it decided not to put the Rev. Umphrey Lee to the test.

III

A Scholar in the Field of Religion

In 1923, when Umphrey Lee was appointed its pastor, the Highland Park Methodist Church South was still the little brown frame church built to meet the needs of Southern Methodist University students who had no transportation to Dallas churches for the required Sunday services, plus a sparse population beginning to move north from downtown Dallas. By 1923, the church had 750 members but inadequate housing and no parsonage. It had paid its pastor $3,600 the previous year.

While a rented house on Haynie Street was being readied, Umphrey and Mary Lee lived with the W. B. Matchett family for several months. This close association ripened into friendship that continued for the remainder of their lives. Mrs. Matchett filled a mother's role with Mary Lee. She was with Mary Lee when her son, Umphrey, Jr., was born. Later the families spent many Colorado vacations together.

The Rev. Umphrey Lee realized that, to be successful at Highland Park Methodist Church, a minister must preach sermons acceptable to varied groups. Students, professional men, businessmen and their wives, Methodists, Baptists, Presbyterians, and presumably an atheist or two, made up the congregation. Some members of the church expressed a fear that a man of thirty was too young and inexperienced to handle the unique problems of this college-community church.

If Umphrey Lee was nervous, as he maintained that he always was before a sermon, he did not show it when he rose to preach his first sermon in the "Little Brown Church" on October 28, 1923. This and subsequent sermons proved to be eminently suitable to the needs of his heterogeneous congregation. The jacket cover of his book *The Bible and Business* states that "students flock regularly to hear him because they know he will not flaunt vagaries about the good, the true, and the beautiful but will speak briefly and to the point about things they understand." For example, Lee once described the Bible in this manner: "The Bible is a book about common people living under the aspect of eternity." (Lee, *Jesus the Pioneer,* p. 17). His sermons "sparkled with humor and logic and scholarship. The hearer did not bat his eye or yawn for fear he would miss a gem." [1]

Often, a brief lesson on the continuity of history and the effect of these events on men's values, hopes, and despairs introduces one of Lee's sermons or books. While his sermons bore the stamp of the classroom lecturer, they were never pedantic. Rather, they were interesting and intelligible to his congregation. They were short, carefully constructed sermons, designed not to resolve but to clarify problems. Many years later, members of his congregation could relate the gist of sermons given in times of public or private crisis. The texts of his sermons support a description of him as "a scholar who happens to be working in the field of religion." [2]

Lee was said almost never to preach a sermon that was not first-rate, and he proved that a scholar could appeal to the man of the world as well as to the man in the church. "Some of his friends think it was symbolic of his life that when he was found stricken in Fondren Library on the day of his death, he was clutching in his hands the proof pages of his last book, *Our Fathers and Us.*" [3]

Umphrey Lee was unquestionably one of the most eloquent,

[1] Doris Miller Johnson, *Golden Prologue to the Future: A History of Highland Park Methodist Church.*
[2] Paul Crume, "SMU Honors First Student President, Now Head of School."
[3] Walter N. Vernon, *Methodism Moves Across North Texas.*

perceptive, and impressive religious leaders ever to have graced the Methodist Church. Much of his greatness rested in his simplicity of style in voicing his beliefs in Christianity. Perhaps he engaged in complicated theological dialogue with his fellow ministers, but in his sermons he omitted discussions of the sophisticated arguments that go on endlessly in some religious groups about doctrines and usages. One of his books explains: "Practical-minded men have difficulty in grasping the convolutions of theological thought when it tries to grapple with problems of sin and redemption, of the nature of man and of God." (Lee, *Our Fathers and Us*, p. 97.) He expounded a compassionate, uncomplicated faith. Doris Miller Johnson pointed out that as pastor of Highland Park Church Dr. Lee was the "wise spokesman" of "this tradition of simple, undogmatic religion." [4]

Lee's idea, as expressed in his sermons, seemed to be that religion is not a means by which one is lulled into a stupor of non-commitment or non-involvement but is, or should be, a means of social adjustment. In *Our Fathers and Us*, he notes that the early Methodist circuit riders preached a "religion of the heart" and consequently were embraced by their uncomplicated pioneer flock. In his books on John Wesley, Dr. Lee points out that this was also true in rural England. Wesley and his preachers did not spend time on theological quandaries; the same may be said about Dr. Lee in his sermons.

Dr. Lee's apparent theological objectivity concealed strong and complex religious feelings. One must read closely to pick out his opinions. Presumably, his selection of quotations contains the key to his ideas, either singly or through progression. His technique was to lead his reader or listener step by step and finally reach an evaluation expressed in his own clever turn of a phrase. His humorous remarks often exposed the

[4] *Golden Prologue to the Future: A History of Highland Park Methodist Church.*

fallacy in a quotation from some authority. One can arrive at many of his own beliefs only by inference, and it would seem that the more important the belief, the more reluctant he was to make a positive statement. The problem or question was meticulously analyzed from all sides and the conclusion left up to the listener or reader.

This characteristically balanced but complex analysis of an issue was illustrated when he observed in a lecture:

> At the present time the most conservative would admit that moral codes are in large part socially determined, and that there is no little relativity in moral ideas. On the other hand, most liberals would now hold that there is moral finality. Like Chesterton, they believe that if you are going to do away with right and wrong you might also dispense with right and left. ("The Spiritual Basis of Democracy," p. 91.)

He had the unique ability of investing old and hackneyed homilies with creative, original phraseology, giving them vitality and relevance for his audience. Dr. Lee reworked these homilies, mottoes, slogans, and proverbs into concise aphorisms appropriate to his topic. He displayed remarkable skill in coining a terse, pithy phrase but never one that was trite or inappropriate. Profundity was never sacrificed for glibness. A clear illustration of phrase-coining is the following:

> Perhaps our fathers spent too much time in learning how to say what they wanted to say, and too little in finding something to say. But their descendants do not improve the situation by having little to say and taking no trouble to say that little well. ("As I See It," Dec. 8, 1957.)

Dr. Lee could give a cliché new vitality: "The old folks used to say that you should count ten before answering when you are mad. Ten was always too short a time to do me much good, but it seems to have been a good average." ("As I See

44

It," September 29, 1957.) Or he could invest an elderly proverb with a youthful twist as when he explained pioneer life as a "world where moral cause and effect seemed fairly obvious," since "He that followed after vain persons had an empty smoke-house; and the field of the slothful cried out that the owner had gone fishing." ("The Preacher and the Modern Mind," p. 3.) No little amount of the credit for his acclaim as a speaker lies in his adroit phraseology.

Dr. Lee not only said it well, but he had something to say; his content matched his form, but one of his well-publicized trademarks was brevity.

Perhaps too much has always been said of Umphrey Lee's predilection for brief sermons, but he did set a new pattern at a time when congregations were used to long and energetic sermons. The widely quoted phrase that Dr. Lee "could say more in ten or fifteen minutes than the average speaker could in twice that time" was not an exaggeration. Lee's philosophic reply to comments on his homiletical brevity was: "No soul was ever saved after the first twenty minutes."

While there was emphasis on brevity, content was never sacrificed for the sake of brevity. He expressed himself with the utmost clarity. Lee's probing, concise speech technique set a standard of excellence in public address for many years in the South and Southwest. Most sermons of other preachers during the period 1923-1936 were thirty minutes to an hour's duration. Some of Dr. Lee's sermons were ten minutes long; the average time was fifteen minutes, and "all during his thirteen years as pastor [at Highland Park Methodist Church] his sermons never exceeded twenty-five minutes." [5]

Dr. Alsup was an elderly member of the congregation at Highland Park. He was a preacher of the old school, known for his one-hour sermons at revival tent meetings. Another church member once commented to Dr. Alsup after one of

[5] Doris Miller Johnson, *Golden Prologue to the Future.*

Dr. Lee's brief sermons, "Well, we heard another fine sermon, didn't we?" Old Dr. Alsup replied, "We certainly did, but I could *kill* him for *quitting!*"

In her history of the Highland Park Church, Mrs. Johnson relates, "The customary rustling that usually followed the opening hymn and prayer had hardly ceased before Umphrey Lee had completed his first sermon. . . . To his startled listeners this brevity came as a complete surprise. It also upset the Sunday dinner schedule, for women knew just how high to leave the stove burning to bring the meal to its best after the sermon." [6]

In Nashville, they still tell of Dr. Lee's first sermon when he became dean of Vanderbilt's School of Religion. "He preached his usual twelve or fifteen minutes and quit. The congregation did not know what to do. They were expecting to stay until twelve o'clock, and they stood around and did not seem to be able to decide whether to go home or not. Church ought not to be this short it seemed." [7]

As a pulpit orator, Dr. Lee was didactic rather than evangelical in his approach, and this was an era in a section of the country which seemed to favor the exhorting style of the evangelist. In fact, some of the older preachers in the North Texas Conference thought he lacked sufficient "hell-fire" in his sermons. Older congregations identified "sermons" with impressive pounding and shouting. One Sunday, while Lee was student pastor in New York City, he preached one of his short, quiet sermons. After the service a lady came up to him and said, "I enjoyed your little *talk*."

While bombast was not typical of Umphrey Lee, his son maintains that he was generously endowed with the vocal equipment to turn up the volume. This he could and did on

[6] *Ibid.*

[7] Walter N. Vernon, *Methodism Moves Across North Texas.*

occasion. Umphrey Lee, Jr. adds that his father, in his later years, humorously observed that he had abandoned such vocal pyrotechnics because of a heart condition, but in his younger preaching days, a vocal blast was of some value in certain situations.

Dr. Lee recalled that at one of his early pastorates an elderly gentleman always sat on the front row, which was fine except that he slept—not only slept, but snored. He snored creatively and with abandon. Finally one Sunday, in exasperation, Lee with all his lung power bellowed, "What this church needs is to wake up!" The old gentleman did just that—arms and legs akimbo with no little agitation, shouting, "Amen."

The Highland Park Church received its full share of attention from both Umphrey and Mary Lee. Giving evidence of his sense of the traditional—Methodism's roots are in the Anglican Church—Umphrey Lee inaugurated the use of the ancient canticles of the service, adding "solemnity and dignity to the church service." "Te Deum," "Venite," and "Jubilate Deo," joined "Bringing in the Sheaves," and "Beulah Land." In addition to selecting personally the hymns for the choir, he also initiated the use of formal choir vestments. Almost as soon as the energetic Lee arrived, he started a program to replace the little brown church with a more imposing edifice.

As pastor of the Highland Park Methodist Church, Umphrey Lee was never an aggressive administrator. Decisions by the board of stewards were strictly by majority vote. "Let's vote on it," was a common phrase. He had ideas and he could suggest, but there was no obvious persuasion. Neither was Dr. Lee energetically social, although no one thought him aloof. But, as one member of the church said, "He could have anything from that church that he wanted." His congregation admired his erudition, believed in his sincerity, was charmed by his sermons and attracted by the warmth of his personality.

47

In the church, at SMU, and in Dallas business circles, acquaintances became and remained friends and admirers.

In his book of sermons, *Jesus the Pioneer,* Umphrey Lee wrote of a conference with the famous Congregational minister Dr. S. Parkes Cadman that could have been the experience of a visitor to Lee's own study:

> I remember calling on Dr. S. Parkes Cadman, the great Brooklyn preacher, when I was a student. I came at one of his office hours and his anteroom was filled with visitors. But there was nothing in Dr. Cadman's inner room to suggest an office. It was more like a study in a private home. I sat and talked with him about my affairs and about other matters for, I thought, at least half an hour. But when I left, I found that I had been talking to him just ten minutes. He had the ability to seem to be taking plenty of time, and to make you feel the same way. This is the quality of unhurried strength which we need to associate with Jesus. (*Jesus the Pioneer,* p. 80.)

Umphrey Lee was the fortunate possessor of a personal magnetism that has come to be called "charisma." It is that mysterious, illusive quality that attracts, fascinates, and influences. It creates a feeling of rapport and inspires loyalty. Charisma seems to be an inherent characteristic that can, perhaps, be enhanced but not created. For instance, most current historians agree that John F. Kennedy was so gifted while Lyndon B. Johnson failed to cultivate even a modicum of the charm that attracts.

This attractiveness is no index to the character of the person. There have been dictators and famous crooks reputed to have possessed the charm and personal persuasiveness that spelled catastrophe for many people. Charisma may be the property of the unscrupulous, the shallow, or the unethical.

Even as a shy, quiet boy and a modest young man Umphrey Lee's presence was felt in any room and any gathering. But he possessed other qualities that guaranteed no later disenchantment. Although intellectually gifted, he was truly a modest, humble man. He had an intuitive understanding of the other person's point of view and a compassionate interest in the welfare of his fellowman. His concern for others, collectively or individually, was real. One of Lee's students in his homiletics class forty years ago remembers vividly Dr. Lee's saying that the most difficult aspect of his ministry was the conducting of funerals. He suffered such emotional trauma empathizing with the family of the deceased that he almost became ill. He was dedicated to his ideals and a persistent, but never belligerent, fighter in any cause. A deeply religious man, he did not separate himself from the world in which he lived.

Without being the organizer, Umphrey Lee tended to be the catalyst of certain part-social, part-serious, part-nonsensical, part-intellectual organizations. If Lee was in attendance, members always left feeling that, in addition to having had an enjoyable time, they had received some intellectual stimulation from their fellow members. One such group in Dallas in the early 1930's called itself "Martha Sumner University." Most members of the group were young professors at Southern Methodist University who later became department heads and deans of the University. They were probably dubbed the young liberals in their day, restive under the restrictions of authority and eager for changes they considered to be progress. The name of the group was taken from the novel *Pigskin* by Charles W. Ferguson, published in 1929, about a mythical school: Martha Sumner University, a barely disguised satire on the Southern Methodist University (SMU) of the 1920's.

One member described it as an "intellectual bonehead club." In a picture taken after one of their bogus initiations, all appear in outlandish garb except the always dignified Umphrey Lee who appears in the very back row, solemn and sedate in suit and, his concession to a costume, an academic gown.

The years at Highland Park Methodist Church were fruitful ones. Lee's output of books was more prolific at that time than later, a consequence of youthful energy sufficient to cope with all demands. Six books were prepared for publication in these thirteen years. In 1925, Cokesbury Press in Nashville, Tennessee, published a thin volume of 115 pages containing twelve of Umphrey Lee's sermons: *Jesus the Pioneer and Other Sermons*. While the young minister's sermons do not contain so many examples of the wit and succinct turn of phrase characteristic of his later speaking and writing, they are brief, fresh, and luminous.

The little book is dedicated "To My Father and Mother." The sermons average less than 2,000 words each and were delivered to the Highland Park Methodist congregation. They are as appropriate and as inspirational today as the day they were written and delivered for the first time.

The key to most of the sermons is to be found in the introduction to the sermon "Open Doors." Lee begins, "One of the richest fruits of the literary study of the Bible is the realization that the books which compose the New Testament were written in definite, concrete situations, to meet definite, concrete human needs." In "The Gospel of Violence" he reiterates, "the setting of the story offers the key to its interpretation."

By explaining the life circumstances in that ancient time, Lee is able to move on to the twentieth-century needs and the application of the Christian doctrine to the satisfaction of those needs. In "The Bread of Life" he emphasizes again, "The fact that Jesus always deals with fundamental human need, that he is the bread of life, reveals his method of approach to human problems." In "The Light of the World": "When we are trying to determine the meaning of Jesus for our modern life, we find it necessary to determine first what he meant for his contemporaries. What did they find in him that satisfied their wants and answered their needs?" The significance for our times is that "Christianity has, in a very real way, pointed out open doors that give new hope and courage to life," and "Christianity has a meaning for our own crowded days in that it does set things in a new perspective. Where we have lost sight of the wood because of the trees, where life has become just one thing after another, and all seems vanity, Christianity offers a new outlook, shows a door that opens out on virgin meadows."

Dr. Lee attempted to provide his congregation at the Highland Park Church with a simplistic approach to living, in contrast to his emphasis on the complexities, in trying to achieve an orderly and socially just world. He was a staunch advocate of the Puritan ethic of work and patience if Christianity would survive in an increasingly secular world. He bemoaned the philosophy of "something for nothing" and the "get-rich-quick" fever. These viewpoints were admirably expressed in a sermon entitled "The Gospel of Violence." He maintained that the contemporary aversion to effort could be seen in our schools in which the students assumed that acquiring an education was comparable to buying a coat. "All that is necessary is that the student pay the bill and appear occasionally for fittings."

He went on to illustrate his thesis, that religion involved effort, by stating that communists held no monopoly on the conception of religion as an opiate of the people. He described a small country church in a prosperous community. Strangely enough, the church was in a sad state of disrepair, but a motto on the wall smugly proclaimed that "The Lord Will Provide." He concluded: "To such people religion is an opiate, drugging them into unconsciousness to the needs of the world and the sorrows of man."

A mastery of homiletic techniques is amply demonstrated in these seemingly plain sermons in *Jesus the Pioneer and Other Sermons*. He made use of thematic words and phrases in a way that never seemed repetitious but achieved unity in presenting his theme. These thematic words or phrases also served to heighten the imagery of his metaphors. In one of his sermons, "mystery" was his key word, and he wove it as a thread connecting his illustrations in the sermon. He described primitive life as being "haunted by mystery." He observed that "an atmosphere of haunting mystery clung to the early idea of God," but social changes had "contributed to this passing of mystery." Not only had modern man lost "his sense of wonder," but he had become "impatient with mystery"; he possessed a "distaste for mystery." In other ages, men "did not shrink from hard wrestling with the problems of the Great Mystery, yet we shrink from and are amazed by the 'mystery of God.' "

According to Lee, "We cannot understand a God who might under some circumstances prefer a yellow man (to say nothing of a black man) to a white." Dr. Lee continued to explore the "great mystery of a loving God and a hard, sometimes cruel world," and then concluded with the central theme of his sermon:

This is the real mystery of God—his love. We shall never know its length and breadth and height and depth; but we must ever be climbing toward it, not as those who have apprehended but as those who have been laid hold on by this intriguing mystery, as those who press forward, confident that

> "The love of God is broader
> Than the measure of man's mind
> And the heart of the Eternal
> Is most wonderfully kind."

("The Darkness of God," *Jesus the Pioneer,* pp. 61-68.)

In the sermon "The Light of the World," Lee noted that "metaphorical language is prominent in the early writings about Jesus." He referred to Jesus as the "Light of the World." He was "The Bread of Life," "The Water of Life," the "Shepherd of the Sheep," "Bright and Morning Star." He further demonstrated his knowledge of figurative language usage when he reminded the listener:

> What cannot be said in ordinary prose is conveyed to us through these metaphors. But to understand these expressions, we must think ourselves back into the position of the men who used the metaphors. And this is not easy to do. Our world is different from their world, and the expressions which retained for them their primitive fringes of meaning have become for us simply literary devices, bare and hackneyed figures of speech. ("The Light of the World," *Jesus the Pioneer*, pp. 69-71.)

Dr. Lee noted that, when men attempt to explain the meaning of the life of Jesus, "we shall have different explanations according to our personal history and according to our mental dispositions." (*Jesus the Pioneer*, p. 9.) He often emphasized the need to understand the language of the Bible in its historical context if we would find relevancy for our lives today. He felt that "the fringes of feeling and attendant images which cling to familiar words are often gone." As an example he cited the metaphor, "Jesus is the Lamb of God." This figure of speech has lost its meaning for moderns because we no longer sacrifice livestock to appease the gods, but the meaning was clear to the ancients. (*Jesus the Pioneer*, p. 2.)

Evidence of his thorough knowledge of etymology, semantics, and his skill in using these disciplines in his rhetoric as supports for a premise was amply demonstrated in these sermons. He often picked a biblical metaphor as an example, such as when he noted that the Moffatt translation from the "Epistle to the Hebrews" utilized the word "leader," instead of "author," as did the King James Version in the passage, "let us run with patience the race that is set before us, looking unto Jesus the leader and perfector of our faith." Lee cited this as an interesting example of the difficulty of conveying an idea by means of word symbols when those words "change their significance through the years." He further maintained that "leader" is the more precise word choice. (*Jesus the Pioneer*, p. 2.)

In these sermons Lee evinced a fondness for alliteration. His writings frequently contained the terms: "priests and prophets." He commented on early Christian communal living: "They pooled their poverty." He described the sophisticated men of the twenties as "tea-table Tarzans." ("*Jesus the Pioneer*, p. 5.)

The year after the publication of *Jesus the Pioneer and Other Sermons*, Josephus Lee, champion of perilous causes, died in a Dallas hospital. He had lived long enough to read his son's first book, dedicated to him and his wife. Josephus Lee had continued to preach almost until his death after forty-seven years of active ministry.

The year before his death, Josephus Lee was protesting with his usual vigor that he had accomplished great things at his Goldthwaite charge "in spite of relentless opposition by the Presiding Elder against every move I made because I would not vote as the Elder wanted on unification" (presumably the unification of the Methodist Church South with the Methodist Church). He listed in a letter to the Presiding Elder and the members of the Quarterly Conference the things he had accomplished that year: he had the best organized church in the district and the best choir; his Sunday school outnumbered the church by thirty; his church had led the district in donations to the orphanage and had bought a Steinway grand piano and a $275 carpet for the church. He added that his church had the largest Wesley Brotherhood in the district, and that a cooperative revival had had over 100 conversions. He felt that he should not have been moved from this charge, but he was approaching his new appointment to Martindale with his usual enthusiasm. Josephus Lee had served such charges in Texas as Zephyr, Blanket, Mansfield, Red Oak, Ferris, Comanche, Santa Anna, Dawson, Marble Falls, and Goldthwaite.

At Goldthwaite a special, sturdy pulpit chair with a double-sized seat was made by a local carpenter to accommodate Josephus Lee's huge bulk. The chair was later presented to his son and was inherited by his grandson. Soon after her husband's death, Esther Lee came to live with the Umphrey Lees and remained with them until her death nearly twenty years later.

On May 16, the cornerstone for the new Highland Park Methodist Church was laid. The building permit, issued in January 1926, estimated the cost to be $325,000. A long time had been spent on the plans. The board of stewards had entrusted the pastor with the authority to choose an architect. The search ended when Roscoe DeWitt, of the firm of DeWitt and Lemmon, submitted a sketch of a Gothic sanctuary.

Both the churchman and the historian in Umphrey Lee responded to the Gothic monuments of the twelfth and thirteenth centuries with their soaring towers, reaching toward heaven, high pointed arches, and dim and peaceful interiors, that tell so much about the pious burghers whose humble shops and homes clustered around their magnificent cathedrals. He was fascinated by the stone carvings and stained-glass windows; he owned a large and impressive volume, *French Cathedral Windows of the Twelfth and Thirteenth Centuries,* by Marcel Aubert. The study of Gothic architecture was continued long after the Highland Park Church was finished and was one of the joys on trips to Europe.

Mr. DeWitt went with Dr. Lee to Chicago and to New York City to investigate church design. New York received much careful inspection since it boasted five or six examples of the Gothic. It was necessary to find some way to adapt the Gothic to its Texas location and to suit the finances of the congregation. The Rev. Umphrey Lee was boldly and prophetically insisting on a sanctuary to seat 1,000 even though the total membership was only about 800 at that time.

Both the architect and the minister had creative inspirations that had to be modified because of cost. Once the basic design was decided upon, they clung to it, hunting ways to save on materials or decoration, or to make temporary substitutions.

Ornamental lettering was substituted for elaborate carving, colored glass was used for a time until the church could afford to replace it with stained glass, quartered white oak was saved to be used for the walls, altar, and doors of the sanctuary while a less expensive wood was used on the ceiling. But nothing was sacrificed that would detract from the solidity or the beauty of the structure. The cost of the Sunday school building and the sanctuary was held to $225,000, and construction of the cloister was postponed until a later more affluent time.

With basic plans decided upon and the cornerstone laid, Umphrey and Mary Lee were free to set off for England in pursuit of the study of John Wesley. For six years Umphrey Lee had dreamed of this trip, and he was not disappointed. The search was rewarding, and Mary Lee was in a happy frame of mind as they traced John Wesley from place to place. The British Museum produced some rare material from the seventeenth and eighteenth centuries. They were excited when they discovered an old iron chest full of original Wesley documents at the Wesleyan Methodist Church in London. The chest was on the floor in the tiny office of the venerable book editor. Umphrey kept remembering the great London fire and was dismayed at such nonchalance about the valuable material.

They made a pilgrimage to Epworth and the old parsonage that was the home of the Wesley family and John Wesley's birthplace, when his father was curate there. The Lees had heard about Jeffrey, the old Jacobite ghost, who was supposed to have snorted when the elder Wesley prayed for the Protestant rulers who were successors to the Catholic sovereigns. John Wesley had believed in this ghost and the present curate did also but, listen as they might, the Lees did not hear him.

The Lees were the amused targets of a little village byplay in the seventeenth-century inn in Epworth. Only tourists attracted by curiosity about John Wesley came to this tiny, out-of-the-way village, and the natives had developed a regular routine of drifting into the inn for a look at the strangers and to have a little "jolly good ale and old." Their conversation, deliberately stout for the benefit of the outsiders, would work around to the question, "Who was this old Wesley I hear so much about?" Another villager would reply, "Oh, he was a lecherous old devil who used to live hereabouts."

John Wesley's burial place in London was visited and, almost on the eve of departure, Lee found out about a history of Methodism written some years before by a Catholic priest in the University of Louvain: *John Wesley: Sa vie et son oeuvre,* par Matthieu Lelièvre. Lee rushed to a bookseller and found that the volume could be obtained but was in French and would have to come from Belgium. Lee had some difficulty convincing the thrifty bookseller, who believed all Americans to be prodigal with their money, that it would be cheaper to spend nine shillings on a cable to have the volume delivered to the steamship than to handle the whole transaction by mail from the United States.

Mary Lee had good reason for casting aside her depression and becoming a joyful companion on this trip. After almost ten years of marriage she had given up hope of having the family she and Umphrey had planned. But they had barely arrived in England when hope was rekindled, and when they met their great friend, the inveterate traveler Virginia Matchett, Mary Lee was so excited and so exuberant that she, inadvertently, also informed all those in the hotel lobby as she rushed to embrace Mrs. Matchett, calling, "I'm pregnant, I'm pregnant." Umphrey Lee, Jr., "Umphs" to his pleased father, was born in Dallas in 1927, when the Lees were living at 3929 Euclid Avenue.

The year 1927 was a satisfying and eventful one for the Lees. On January 24, Umphrey, Jr. was born. The next month the new church was ready for its first service, and church membership had risen to 1,398. In May, Umphrey Lee received his first honorary degree, the D.D., from Trinity University. In September, Umphrey Lee became officially connected with SMU for the third time, when he was appointed professor of homiletics in the School of Theology, adding formal graduate school teaching, for the next five years, to his Men's Bible Class, his preaching and pastoral duties, civic work, and other heavy demands as he became a popular community speaker. Addressing the SMU convocation, Professor Lee advised the students, "You accept the universe because you can't help it. Thus there are certain things that must be accepted. By getting rid of the immediate difficulties you can do the things you want to." [8]

In addition to his other activities, Dr. Lee completed the manuscript of *The Lord's Horseman: John Wesley,* that was to be published the next year, and he could, then, devote more time to the scholarly work that was to be his dissertation for the Ph.D degree.

The last details for the new church were being finished. Much of the artistic, decorative work was done in Dallas by local artisans. Members made gifts of special fittings and appointments. Mary Lee gave the communion table in memory of her mother. The completed Highland Park Methodist Church reflected the dignity, sincere faith, and comforting devotion of the man who planned it with such care.

[8] *The Campus,* December 3, 1927.

It was described as an adaptation of late Gothic to modern needs. The vaulted ceiling of the auditorium with its great beams was reminiscent of the great parish churches of England. High windows were an admirable adaptation of perpendicular Gothic for a southern climate where too much light is to be avoided. Colored (later, stained) glass windows were of floral and geometric design in brilliant blues, soft yellow, rose, and green. Small touches of bright red and bright green admitted soft but adequate light and tracery that recalled the late development of Gothic architecture. The arrangement of pulpit, font, and table was in accordance with good Protestant tradition in which preaching the Word is ranked along with the administration of the Lord's supper and baptism.

IV

The Lord's Horseman

The fruit of eight years of labor, *The Lord's Horseman: John Wesley,* was finally published in 1928. A penetrating biographical study, it brought unexpected prestige to Dr. Lee. Much material had been published about Wesley, but this interpretation was unique because it did not picture John Wesley as a "stained-glass saint" but as a living, human prophet. Following the same historical approach prominent in *Jesus the Pioneer and Other Sermons,* Lee indicated in the preface of *The Lord's Horseman:* "The purpose of this volume is to portray Wesley in the perspective of his own time . . . and to remember that he was a man."

He traced Wesley's development, education, love affairs, conversion, and the unfolding of the Methodist movement. This life story of John Wesley, who "never meant to found" the Methodist Church but is remembered for nothing else, begins with his birth to the Anglican clergyman Samuel Wesley and his wife Susanna Annesley, in the old rectory at Epworth in 1703, and ends with Wesley's death in London in 1791. Dr. Lee observed that men who survived Wesley built a church on the foundations laid by John Wesley, but Lee indicated that Wesley might not have given total approval had he been able to see the result. Lee went on to say: "But the catholic-minded man, who had dreamed of a new world in which men might adventure in the spirit without clash of creeds, was dead; and what he would have thought and said of the work of his successors, no one will ever know."

How did the Methodists come to be known as "Methodists"?

According to Lee in *The Lord's Horseman,* Wesley, when he was in Oxford in 1729, organized a small group of students of a religious nature, the "Holy Club." They all embraced the Calvinistic doctrines of work, discipline, and frugality. The small band was dedicated to marching together to sacramental services. In order to save money, some, along with their leader John Wesley, wore their hair long. They renounced worldly goods and assiduously observed "puritanic abstinence from even innocent pleasures; and, not hesitating, rebuked all who differed from them." Such actions invited their being dubbed, among other epithets, "Bible Moths," "Holy Club," and at last, "Methodists."

The book further explained:

The name, which had been used in the seventeenth century to designate methodical people, was quickly taken up, and Methodists the followers of John Wesley remain to this day. . . . They endured this obloquy, perhaps enjoying this feeling of martyrdom which is the luxury of the young and the obsession of the fanatic. . . . "You must be singular or be damned," said their leader; and the Methodists were both singular and heartily damned by the rest of the University. (*The Lord's Horseman,* pp. 36-37.)

But Dr. Lee stated that, while the members of this Oxford group were important in the leadership of the evangelical movement called "Methodism," the true Methodist revival began after the "conversion" of John Wesley in Aldersgate Street in 1738. Later Lee wrote that this "marked for him a religious experience, epochal for his later preaching," (*Historical Backgrounds of Early Methodist Enthusiasm,* p. 120) and, in *John Wesley and Modern Religion,* he further explains his own interpretation of the Aldersgate experience as a mystical and not an evangelical conversion. "The conversion of a religious man to a higher state of religious devotion. . . . Aldersgate marked a stage in his religious experience, and a

61

very important stage; but it was neither the beginning of the Christian life nor the end of it."

The essence of the Aldersgate experience was the "conviction that the pardoning love of God was individual for one's self and something whose realization was powerful in one's life. It is this conviction that he has loved *me* and saved *me*. . . . It is this conviction and its importance for present salvation that is the essence of the Methodist preaching of justification by faith." (*Our Fathers and Us,* p. 55.)

Lee's emphasis upon the eighteenth century's perspective was an original approach for the time, 1928. It was for this reason that he included the two little-known documents which appeared in the appendices in the 1928 edition of the book. The documents give a vivid description of Wesley's love affair with Grace Murray and later his unhappy relationship with his wife Molly, the former Mrs. Vazeille, a merchant's widow.

Wesley's prose was in typical eighteenth-century style. In flowing rhetoric, Wesley recorded for posterity that Grace Murray often accompanied him on his preaching tours of the English countryside. They traveled by horseback, and Wesley noted that Grace Murray "greatly assists and furthers me in my work, enlivening my dull and dead affections, composing and calming my hurried thoughts, . . . at the same time loosening my soul from all below, and raising it up to God." In another place, in Wesley's wordy description of this long drawn-out and turbulent love affair, he wrote, "Every hour gave me fresh proof of her usefulness on the one hand and her affection on the other. Yet I could not consent to her repeated request to marry immediately." (*The Lord's Horseman,* 1928 edition, p. 326 and p. 279.)

Lee and his publishers came to feel that discretion was the better part of scholarship in spite of the fact that the documents did much to humanize the heretofore austere conception of Wesley. *The Saturday Review of Literature* praised Lee's "good sense" in understanding that Wesley's love affairs, "while vivid and engrossing, are really of secondary importance in estimating the man," and added that it was for this reason that Lee called them "Interlude" and put them in the appendices. The reviewer in the same publication further supported the inclusion of the Wesley papers by describing them as "moving, vivid, and psychologically important documents, nowhere else generally available, at least so far as this reviewer knows, in their unadorned entirety." [1]

In an interview immediately after the release of the book, Lee explained that the attitude of biographers and readers had changed toward figures of the past so that intimate psychological revelations of Wesley's "profane" loves, as well as "sacred" love, largely from the pen of Wesley himself, could be used as they could not have been in the past when they "simply would have burst the bounds of strict mid-Victorian conventionality." [2] Umphrey Lee found, to his dismay, that he was still a little ahead of his time. The offending documents were deleted from a later edition of his book.

On the occasion of the publication of the revised edition of *The Lord's Horseman: John Wesley,* the book was described as "A standard since its first publication twenty-five years ago." (*The Christian Century,* December 22, 1954.) When the first edition of the book was published in 1928, R. L. Calhoun in the *Yale Review* commented on Lee's skill as a writer of clear, intelligible prose. (Autumn 1929, p. 197.) The *Boston Transcript* emphasized that Lee had successfully depicted the "human qualities" of John Wesley. The laudatory nature of the reviews was climaxed by the *Bookman* which observed that Lee had written an "engaging and original story of a man who would undoubtedly be pleased with the finished work." The reviewer went on to praise Lee's good taste and manners which

---

[1] B. L. Bell, *The Saturday Review of Literature,* January 26, 1929.
[2] Sam Acheson, "Dallas Pastor's Biography of Founder of Methodism."

were described as above the level of most biographers of the day, and noted that Lee might serve well for those "chroniclers who feel that they have no function in life but to debunk and to denude." (January 1929.)

However, all was not hosannas. A pejorative cry of dissent was raised by the *Journal of Religion* which chided, "In so brief an account of John Wesley it is certainly poor judgment and perhaps poorer taste to lug in so much of the type of material which smacks of sex appeal." (January 1929.)

Dr. Lee's interest in speech techniques and their application was shown by his inclusion of a detailed analysis of Wesley's rhetorical style. He described Wesley's pulpit prose as having its strength in its simplicity, "delivered with piercing directness." (*The Lord's Horseman*, p. 92.)

As a young rector, John Wesley felt that his restless congregation was not grasping the meaning in his sermons. To correct this, Wesley asked a maid in the household to listen to him read one of his sermons. The maid was to "stop him at every word she did not understand. . . . Her, 'Stop, Sir' came annoyingly often, but every time Wesley resolutely substituted an easy word for a hard one." Lee followed the example set by Wesley and the apparent simplicity of his speeches was, in reality, an example of fine craftsmanship.

According to Lee, the following incident, perhaps apocryphal, transpired in Wesley's youth:

An usher once found him haranguing a group of smaller boys, and inquired of the orator why he chose to associate with lower-form boys rather than with older pupils. Young Wesley's reply was oracular: "Better to rule in hell than to serve in heaven." (*The Lord's Horseman*, p. 15.)

This human quality of Wesley intrigued Lee as much as the Wesleyan theology. Unlike many scholars Dr. Lee had a sense

64

of humor in regard to his particular field. In one of his Fondren Lectures at SMU, he once commented on the voluminous diaries in which Wesley probed his inner motivation: "John Wesley was always pulling his soul up by the roots to see how it was growing."

In the same lecture, he remarked on Wesley's habit of moving his preachers from a parish after a short time. "Otherwise, they wore themselves out and most of their audience. They ran out of material."

Like Lee, Wesley was not devoid of humor; indeed Wesley possessed a wit that rivaled the droll humor of his biographer. Lee related an incident when Wesley and one of his preachers were dining with a friend. Wesley's preacher charge remarked on the abundance of food and added that it seemed hardly an example of self-denial. "Wesley quietly suggested that the loaded table offered the perturbed preacher a most excellent opportunity to practice that virtue." (*The Lord's Horseman*, pp. 143-44.)

Lee surmised that Wesley's delicate health in his youth probably directed his attention to medicine. The subject Wesley attacked with evangelistic zeal, as he did any subject which interested him. Wesley wrote a book on medicine, which he revised and enlarged many times in a forty-three-year period. In the year of his death, the twenty-third edition was published. There are many curious prescriptions advanced by Wesley in the book, entitled *Primitive Physick: or an Easy and Natural Method of Curing Most Diseases*. Wesley recommended the following for "a consumption":

Take a cowheel from the Tripe-house ready drest, two quarts of new milk, two ounces of Hartshorn shavings, two ounces of Isinglass, a quarter of a pound of Sugar-candy, and a Race of Ginger. Put all these in a Pot; and set them in an Oven after the Bread is drawn . . . ; and let the Patient live on this.

Lee observed that most of Wesley's prescriptions were simpler. For "Raging Madness," Wesley advised tersely, "Let him eat nothing but apples for a month." Lee carefully explained that Wesley's medical advice was not exceedingly strange but was quite in keeping with the medical knowledge of the eighteenth century.

In defense of John Wesley's failure to accept fully Newton's discoveries or the Copernican theory, Lee pointed out in a review of another book on John Wesley that in Wesley's England scientists did not enjoy the benefits of modern press agentries: "Einstein would not have been annoyed by autograph hunters." [3]

The acclaim accorded *The Lord's Horseman* was gratifying but creativity required nourishment. For the tremendous output of sermons, speeches, articles, and books, Dr. Lee constantly sought illumination, wisdom, and inspiration. He was avid for more information about John Wesley. There was always stimulation and enlightenment in gazing at his favorite Gothic churches in Europe. He was eager to complete work toward the Ph.D. degree at Columbia and wanted another look at Wesley documents in the British Museum, so he asked for a leave of absence to begin in September 1928. President Charles C. Selecman and Vice President Horace M. Whaling of Southern Methodist University agreed to occupy his pulpit in his absence. *The Campus,* in announcing Lee's imminent departure, added, apropos of nothing, "Dr. Lee is a liberal thinker," apparently intending it as a compliment.

The Lee family set out for New York and again were fascinated by the cosmopolitan air of the big city. During the winter Umphrey Lee completed all degree requirements at Columbia, except the dissertation, and continued his research at Columbia and in various New York libraries. Then he and two friends

[3] Lee, Review of *John Wesley,* by Francis J. McConnell, *Religion in Life,* Autumn 1939.

sailed for Europe. Companions were Ora Miner, Southern Methodist University Professor of Town and Country Churches, and William G. Birkner, a theology student at SMU.

Dr. Lee liked to travel, to savor old cultures, great literature, and the charm of old churches. The religious and social life of the past, as reflected in the famous cathedrals of Europe, fascinated the historian Umphrey Lee, and he was captivated and inspired by the beauty of ancient architecture in its natural setting on the European continent. The three travelers visited cathedrals in Amiens, Rouen, Caen, Bayeux, Constance, and Mont St. Michel. Professor Miner took many pictures. When their pilgrimage ended, Mr. Birkner made a leisurely trip home on a freighter while Professors Lee and Miner returned together on a passenger ship and were back in Dallas for the opening of the fall session of SMU in September 1929.

Before their return, Dr. Lee's small book, *The Life of Christ: A Brief Outline for Students,* was off the press. The structure of this text with its clear outlines, study guides, simple presentation, and clever repetitions marks the author as the excellent teacher his students reported him to be.

The Lees settled into their third Dallas parsonage, this time at 3417 University Boulevard. The Highland Park Methodist Church was now paying its pastor $6,000 a year. The Lees had shared in the general euphoria that had permeated the United States through the years of soaring prosperity after World War I. The last years had been good and the future appeared rosy, but the shattering of the dream of continuing prosperity came in October 1929. On the twenty-first, stocks began to sag and on the twenty-ninth came the catastrophic crash that was the culmination of a boom market and unrestrained speculation of the 1920's.

The country was unprepared and the first reaction was one of shocked incredulity. Repercussions in unemployment, bank failures, and business disasters were felt almost immediately in the East but, for a time, the Dallas area remained almost untouched as the panic moved relentlessly westward.

Umphrey Lee had returned to his usual activities as pastor of the Highland Park Methodist Church, resumed teaching his classes at Southern Methodist University, teaching his Men's Bible Class at the Sunday school, and participating again in many civic projects, but he still found time to write. From the time he entered graduate school until the day of his death Umphrey Lee was overwhelmed with ideas he wished to investigate and develop into books. He worked on several potential publications simultaneously. Beginning in 1929, a Lee book came off the press each year for four years.

In 1930, *The Bible and Business,* based on lectures to his Men's Bible Class, was released. In it Lee voiced what he considered to be the Christian ethic as related to the economy or, more specifically, to modern western man's reverence for property and wealth. He noted that Jesus considered the man who amassed wealth and property for selfish purposes as a fool; furthermore, Jesus, according to Lee, felt wealth to be a "moral danger" as a wealthy man becomes a slave to his possessions. He emphasized that "Jesus says emphatically that a rich man can be saved by the grace of God; but he implies that it will take just that." (*The Bible and Business,* pp. 107-9, 164.) He based his conclusions on Matthew 6:25 and Mark 10:27.

In writing this treatise, historian Lee must have had a delightful time tracing the development of business practices, business ethics, and business vocabulary through changing biblical periods. In his careful, thorough way he distilled the "essential problems of man's relation to his fellows" in desert, country, or city, emphasizing again that writers of the Bible were writing for their own day and own problems, but that true worth is in the principles by which man can meet new conditions and still preserve fundamental values.

Commenting on the complexities of modern life and how

the size of business organizations tend to de-emphasize the individual, Lee ends:

Whether these kingdoms of the world will be subordinated to human needs is a question. . . . If the task is accomplished, it will not be by exhortation but by social engineering; and to promote it religion will have to muster all the resources at her call. Not least among these resources will be the living testimony of the Book, which here standeth sure for all men of good will, that all economic organizations must aim at justice and that man's soul must not be in slavery to the things he possesseth. (*The Bible and Business,* p. 164.)

Another bright spot in the troublesome early depression years was the completion of graduate work and notification that the Ph.D. would be awarded by Columbia University. Lee left for New York on Monday, February 16, 1931, and returned later in the week a full-fledged Ph.D. It had taken him more than ten years to achieve this goal. "Papa" had died before Umphrey had fulfilled "his dearest wish" but by the time of his father's death, the degree was in sight, and Josephus Lee could foresee a bright future for his favorite son. The doctoral dissertation, finally entitled *The Historical Backgrounds of Early Methodist Enthusiasm,* was published by the Columbia University Press in 1931, and was dedicated to "My Father."

Long hours of tedious research had gone into this thesis. Dr. Lee liked to relate, humorously, that even the title had not been decided offhandedly. His advisory professor at Columbia recommended that he entitle his book: *Historical Backgrounds of Methodist Enthusiasm.* Lee thought the title should have more "pep." Furthermore, Lee didn't believe that such a title "would appeal to the average reader." "I'll think it over," said the professor solemnly. A short time later the professor called Lee and very excitedly exclaimed, "I have it, Lee! We'll call your book *Historical Backgrounds of* EARLY *Methodist Enthusiasm."*

This scholarly work, as befits a Ph.D. dissertation, abounds in references and evidences of the meticulous, painstaking research done both in this country and in England. It traces the attitude of society toward prophecy, mysticism, divine revelation or "the claim to immediate inspiration" (*John Wesley and Modern Religion,* p. 37) from Greek theories of inspiration through the seventeenth and eighteenth centuries and, specifically, during the time of the beginning Methodist movement. References include scarce and rare items consulted in the British Museum such as volumes by Jacob Bauthumley, 1650; Robert Barclay, 1676; Samuel Annesley, 1683; Edmund Chishull, 1708; Henry Nicholson, 1708; and Frances Atterbury, 1710.

With this work Dr. Lee gained definite status as a scholar. A. W. Harrison, writing in the *Proceedings of the Wesley Historical Society,* cited Dr. Lee as authority for his statement that enthusiasm is used in a good sense today but had undesirable significance in the eighteenth century when "any increase in zeal, in fervor or devotion, any marked carefulness of living was enthusiasm," and any excess of religious excitement was feared.

By the fall of 1931, rumblings of the stock market crash had reached Dallas and the Highland Park Methodist Church. In the October church bulletin Dr. Lee wrote:

Since the strict economy at this time requires that we dispense with weekly bulletins, I am handing you this booklet in order that you may have certain information about your church as we come to the end of the conference year. For the benefit of insomnia sufferers, I have added a sermon.

The booklet was mimeographed and carried the postscript, "This is not paid out of church funds." The church was then faced with a $13,000 payment on church bonds. Credit was given to Dr. Lee's genius and the many devoted members of the congregation who not only saved the church financially but enabled it to meet its commitment to the North Texas Conference during the depression years.

The years 1930-1934 were turbulent years in the North Texas Conference of the Methodist Church South, and even one as adept as Umphrey Lee could not remain aloof from the power struggle going on in all echelons of the conference. The difficulties began with personal animosities and were probably accentuated by the depression and the precarious financial situation. A remark made by one member of the conference about two ministerial associates started the conflagration. As the antagonisms grew and developed into a power struggle, with the better-paying pastorates and honored positions as the prizes, members of the conference were inevitably forced to take sides, and neutrality became impossible.

As the struggle reached the crisis stage, the lines became clearly delineated. One faction was headed by President Selecman of Southern Methodist University, Bishop H. A. Boaz, and Dr. Frank M. Richardson, who had made the original unfortunate remark about the Rev. S. A. Barnes and the Rev. Harold G. Cook. The Rev. S. A. Barnes and others, obviously, made up the other faction.

Dr. Lee, a man who would not compromise his principles but recoiled from any sort of unpleasantness, found himself in an untenable position. He was never publicly allied with either faction, but it was known that his sympathies were with the Barnes group, and he played a limited role behind the scenes. When it came time to elect delegates to the next General Conference, he was one of the eight clerical delegates proposed and elected by those in opposition to President Selecman.

Deadly animosities grew out of these unfortunate years, and some wounds were never healed. Major and minor affairs of

71

the conference became involved and opinions polarized. Affected were Southern Methodist University, the presiding eldership, pastoral assignments, and delegations to the General Conference.

In October 1932, Bishop H. A. Boaz announced that Umphrey Lee would be transferred at the end of the conference year, possibly to a pulpit somewhere in the East. President Selecman was already teaching Lee's classes in the School of Theology at SMU.

The hopeless wrangles and feuds in the conference had made Umphrey Lee feel, too, that he should leave the North Texas Conference and, if possible, find a more peaceful atmosphere in which to work. But many people in his congregation and in Dallas urged him to remain. Students at SMU quickly circulated a petition asking him to continue in Dallas, and protests came from many other groups. In a few days, the Dallas papers announced that Dr. Lee would not be transferred from the Highland Park Methodist Church but would take a year's leave instead, and that his old friend from SMU college days, Dr. Robert W. Goodloe, now professor of church history in the SMU School of Theology, had been named to fill the pulpit vacated during the sabbatical leave. The announcement was made by Eugene McElvaney, chairman of the board of stewards of the church.

Dr. and Mrs. Lee, with five-year-old Umphrey, Jr., sailed on the Cunard Line's RMS Franconia prepared for another profitable visit to Europe. They planned to stay a year. Dr. Lee felt that the trip would give him an opportunity to make a more objective decision about the conference and his future in it, as well as provide surcease from the strain of the last years and time for a relaxing holiday with his family.

They were in London on November 12, 1932, but the start of their gala year had not been auspicious. The crossing was rough and "Umphs" was ill with a severe cold all the way over, so they stayed on the ship instead of disembarking at Le Havre for the train trip to Paris as they had planned. During the winter, financial reports from the United States worried the Lees, but they went on to Germany where Umphrey had planned some special study.

They were on hand to see the final decline and fall of the Weimar Republic. Conditions in Germany were chaotic. The disaster of World War I was not forgotten, and Germany had never really recovered from the desperate, inflation-ridden years immediately after the war. For a few years the democratic Weimar Republic gained popularity, economic conditions improved, and American loans helped her to make reparations payments. Then came the crash of 1929 that triggered a depression in Europe as well as in the United States. The Weimar Republic could not cope with the economic debacle.

Out of the confusion and desperation rose the National-Socialist (Nazi) Party to a position of importance. In January 1933, Hitler and his party commanded a parliamentary majority, and the senile president, Field-Marshall Hindenburg, appointed him chancellor. Hitler moved swiftly, and within a few months all opposition was crushed.

In Berlin, soon after Hitler's appointment as chancellor, Dr. Lee had the experience later reported by Frank X. Tolbert:

Dr. Lee is probably the only college president in the country who has been tossed, bodily, out of an athletic stadium. The scene of this eviction was Berlin's gigantic Sportspalast. The time was Spring, 1933. Hitler had just made a speech and was leaving the stadium. Everyone stood up and cheered and raised arms in Nazi salutes. Everyone, that is, but Lee and his three companions.

"A bunch of brown-shirted SS troops charged us," said Lee. Two of his companions, a Welsh newspaper correspondent and an American reporter, were badly beaten. Dr. Lee was only shoved out of the stadium.

"I stood there for a few minutes until the brown shirts had gone.

And I thought: I've paid for that seat, Hitler charged admission to his speeches. Also, I thought: I'm here in Berlin as a student. This is something no student should miss."

So Umphrey Lee walked back into the Sportspalast.[4]

By the second of March, the Lees, observing the hysterical conditions in Germany and reading of the situation at home, became thoroughly frightened and made plans to leave Berlin for the United States on March 9. At the same time he had written to R. H. Shuttles, chairman of the board of trustees at SMU and prominent in the Highland Park Methodist Church, about the possibility of returning to Dallas before his year's leave of absence was up.

Franklin D. Roosevelt had been inaugurated as President of the United States on March 4, and the next day took the drastic emergency measure of closing the banks until some order could be established out of the economic chaos. Mr. Shuttles did not receive the letter from Lee until the next day, March 6, and delayed a definite answer to Lee's questions for another ten days. Meanwhile he and Miss Margaret Todd, Dr. Lee's secretary, reassured the Lees, as friends alone in a strange land, by a cable saying that everyone was calm and the banks expected to open shortly.

By March 17, Mr. Shuttles could write cheerfully, care of the SS "City of Baltimore," that all were eager for Dr. Lee to return, that Dr. Goodloe was perfectly agreeable to Dr. Lee's taking back his pulpit, and that he had heard that Bishop J. M. Moore intended offering Lee the deanship of the Southern Methodist School of Theology. Mr. Shuttles added that he had told Bishop Moore that he knew Dr. Lee would not be interested, as long as the present head (of SMU) continued, referring to the known friction between Umphrey Lee and President Selecman.

[4] Frank X. Tolbert, "Headliner Portrait."

74

Home to 3417 University Boulevard, Dallas, Dr. Lee again took up his activities at the church and in the city of Dallas.

As mentioned previously, at the annual meeting of the North Texas Conference in Denison in October 1933, Dr. Lee was chosen one of the eight clerical delegates to the General Conference of the Methodist Church South which was to meet the next year. Lee had transferred to the North Texas Conference in 1923 when he had come to the Dallas church. For the first few years the journals of the conference do not list Lee as serving on committees or speaking at any of the sessions. It can be assumed that he maintained a modest silence as a youthful newcomer. After three years in the conference he was appointed on a special committee dealing with the Wesley Foundation of Texas and the Wesley Bible Chair at the University of Texas.

In 1930, his name began to appear each year on permanent and temporary committees. When there was a resolution to assuage or to compliment, Umphrey Lee's name led all the rest. If an innovation was proposed, Umphrey Lee was on the committee to investigate. Perhaps it was he who had called attention to the needs that led to The Committee to Plan for an Historical Society, The Committee on an Annuity Insurance Plan, The Committee on the Methodist Centennial, and others. For many years he was active in encouraging financial support for Methodist colleges and universities. Some years he served on several committees.

Dr. Lee was chairman of the Board of Christian Literature for nine years. In 1935, he reported that, in spite of generally adverse business conditions, the Methodist Publishing House showed a profit of more than $60,000 from Sunday school periodicals, the *Christian Advocate,* etc. Unlike his sermons, his report was lengthy, praising editors and laying out a business like plan to increase subscribers and users of publications. In 1939, after the union with the other Methodist

75

churches, Dr. Lee ended his final report: "As this is the last report of your Board of Christian Literature in the Methodist Church South, it has been spoken of as a 'swan song.' We like to think of it as 'the song of the lark' for we see in our united Methodist Church the dawn of a new day!" [5]

From 1930, Dr. Lee's prominence and influence in the conference increased. The Methodist Church holds a general conference every four years. Umphrey Lee was a delegate from the North Texas Conference four times, 1934, 1940, 1944, 1948. He was a member of the uniting conference in 1939 and of the ecumenical conferences in 1946 and 1951. "Considering all aspects of conference life, he [Umphrey Lee] was perhaps the most influential member of the conference during the years from 1930 to 1955." [6]

In 1936, Dr. Lee's stature as a noted Wesleyan authority was increased by the publication of *John Wesley and Modern Religion*. This study portrayed the unwitting founder of Methodism in the light of his own century, emphasizing that Wesley should be understood and evaluated in terms of his own time and not by standards developed in changed nineteenth- or twentieth-century conditions. This was Lee's typical historical approach, often repeated. The author identified the dual tendencies in Wesley's nature (discipline, order, conformity versus the romantic and poetic) and an intellect of "breadth and depth" which could not be "easily cramped into single doctrinal formulas."

Lee's research and interpretation helped Methodists to rethink the Wesleyan doctrines of conversion, sanctification, and Christian perfection. Dr. Lee stated that Wesley clearly indicated that "Christian perfection is an ideal not to be obtained but by the grace of God." (*John Wesley and Modern Religion,* pp. 72-73.)

[5] *Journal of the North Texas Conference,* 1939, p. 45.
[6] Walter N. Vernon, *Methodism Moves Across North Texas.*

W. E. Sangster, an English Wesleyan historian, noted in his book on Wesley, *The Path to Perfection,* that he and Dr. Lee were in agreement with Dr. G. C. Cell's statement that Wesley's doctrine is a "unique synthesis of the Protestant ethic of grace with the Catholic ethic of holiness." Yet another theologian, Robert C. Monk, observed:

Scholars have spent much energy in the past quarter century attempting to determine the relationship of justification and sanctification in Wesley's theology. Those favoring a Catholic (or Anglican) interpretation, such as Maximin Piette and Umphrey Lee, have insisted upon the dominant role of sanctification.[7]

In his last book, *Our Fathers and Us,* published twenty-seven years later, Dr. Lee continues the interpretation begun in *John Wesley and Modern Religion:*

When Wesley talks about salvation he is talking about two different kinds of salvation: present and final. For present salvation a man must have a sure trust and confidence. For final salvation there must be holiness of life achieved by faith during man's lifetime or in the hour and article of death—but holiness there must be. (*Our Fathers and Us,* p. 59.)

Dr. Lee also held firmly to the feeling that man has a role to play in salvation, and that Wesley taught this. He quotes Wesley: "Undoubtedly faith is the work of God, and yet it is the duty of man to believe. And every man may believe if he will. . . . Believing is the act of the human mind, strengthened by the power of God." (*Our Fathers and Us,* p. 77.) In the same book, Dr. Lee continues:

We have perhaps been guilty of careless thinking and undue emphasis upon works, as if they alone could merit our salvation. . . .

[7] Robert C. Monk, *John Wesley and His Puritan Heritage.*

But it might as well be understood that actually the Methodists have grounds for their belief in the importance of good works. Our notion of good works and eighteenth-century notions may not coincide, but there is no question whatsoever that during all his life Wesley insisted that man could resist the Spirit of God if he chose to do so. (P. 79.)

The implication here is that if man chooses whether or not to yield to God's Spirit, then he has a definite role to play in his salvation. Of course, he does not save himself for "he [Wesley] at least makes it clear that he is not preaching that men may of their own efforts achieve salvation . . . ; that man must find salvation through the Grace of God." He could also offer a solution to man's polylemma: "informed confidence, . . . people who know what they believe." (Lee, "The Community of the Confident," *The Methodist Hour,* January 19, 1947.)

Along with Wesley, Lee realized the need, the "psychological value of humble faith." (*John Wesley and Modern Religion,* p. 81.) On another occasion, he told a symposium of historians, "If fashions in history . . . reveal the essence of modern man's loneliness, they reveal also some of the limitations of history." He went on to remind them: "It is well to remember that the faith which was meaningful in the Western world was not faith in the abstract law, but in a Being with humane qualities." ("History and the Intellectual Climate," *Integration of the Humanities and the Social Sciences:* A Symposium, p. 44.)

Speaking of the intensity of the emotional reactions manifested in early Methodist meetings, Dr. Lee points out the psychological conditions; the great crowds; the singing of both joyful hymns and songs filled with sorrow in quick succession; the emotionally charged sermons; the prayers of exhortation that made the crowds highly suggestible to demonstrations of a violent nature; but he adds, "one must not forget, too, the often demonstrated power of the Christian story over the minds and hearts of men. The elemental drama of the life and death of Jesus has for centuries been the most deeply affecting of all of mankind's stories." (*John Wesley and Modern Religion,* p. 287.)

Lee seemed to feel that the contribution of Wesley and the early Methodists to the "breakdown of the older orthodoxy and rationalism was in their emphasis upon a milder conception of God, upon Christian experience as taking precedence over dogma, and in their stress upon feeling." (P. 302.)

In the following pages the author maintained, in 1936, that "little sense of the awfulness of God" remained in sections of Protestantism:

If the God of Calvinism is dead, his place has been taken by an Indulgent Being who is surprisingly like a complacent American father; . . . modern man has awakened to the fact that God has been lost in the Universe of which man is so small a part. And man, the magnificent conqueror of the nineteenth century, has been lost also. (Pp. 307-10.)

Again the Methodist historian's efforts met with critical success. His writing was described as scholarly, authoritative, and definitive. Lee was depicted as having "an impeccable standard of historical judgment," and the fruit of that judgment was described as "a work of first-class importance in the field of religion." [8]

A review of *John Wesley and Modern Religion* in *Religion in Life* calls the book "brilliant," points out that Lee "dug up new and conclusive evidence." It continues: "This

[8] J. H. Holmes, *Books,* October 4, 1936.

book, as no other, rescues Wesley from the fog and mists of antiquity and gives us the real man against the background of his own time . . . and of our own. Furthermore, the work is couched in admirable literary style, abounding in epigrammatic expressions and witty characterizations which the delighted reviewer can scarce forbear to quote." [9]

Dr. Lee's definitive studies of Wesley were respected, not only in America but in Europe. He was said to write "religious history books that even atheists find readable." His good friend and associate, Dr. Herbert Gambrell, wrote in the Memorial preface to *Our Fathers and Us* that, although he was "trained in rigidly Calvinistic colleges, he became one of the great interpreters of the Arminian tradition and of the Wesleyan movement." Harold Lindstrom, noted Swedish religious historian, besides quoting Lee in his own book, *Wesley and Sanctification: A Study of the Doctrine of Salvation,* wrote that Lee found the thing which gave Wesley his place in history—"his combination of mystical experience with the ethical, the rational, and the institutional elements in religion."

The name of Lee began to appear frequently as the authority for any statement about John Wesley. Bishop Francis J. McConnell identified him as authority for stating that Samuel Wesley was a strict disciplinarian in ecclesiastical requirements. A. W. Harrison referred to Lee as one who "is well-known as the author of *The Lord's Horseman.*" Reviewers were generally extravagant in praise of both books on John Wesley, remarking upon the scholarship, style, and taste.

In the spring of 1936, Dr. Lee was offered the deanship of the School of Religion at Vanderbilt University, Nashville, Tennessee, which he accepted. He left the Highland Park Methodist Church with great reluctance. His sermons there

[9] James R. Joy in *Religion in Life,* Winter 1937, pp. 314-15.

had drawn an ever-increasing congregation. In the fall of 1936 the conference report listed a membership of 2,349. The number had tripled since he had come to the church in 1923. The congregation and Dr. Lee were finishing thirteen years of rewarding association.

V

"Glad YOU Could Be with US"

Part of the attraction of Vanderbilt University was that Dr. Lee would teach; for, in addition to the deanship of the School of Religion, he was also to hold the position of Drucilla Moore Buffington Professor of Church History. He was to assume the new position in early summer. There was a flurry of preparations to move; friends who came to express regrets; an alumni dinner on the SMU campus presided over by university officers, honoring Dr. and Mrs. Lee; farewell dinners; and a last sermon to preach at Highland Park Methodist Church on June 14, 1936.

Nothing can more clearly illustrate Umphrey Lee's lack of personal vanity than his continually telling stories which turned the humor on himself. He not only enjoyed a bit of humor at his own expense, he could perpetuate it. Two such stories deal with his introduction to Vanderbilt:

The aged chancellor of Vanderbilt, Dr. James H. Kirkland, came out of his retirement to welcome the new dean of the School of Religion.

"I'm delighted you could be with us, Dr. Kirkland," said Umphrey Lee in greeting.

"Humph! I belong here, young sprout! Glad *you* could be with us." [1]

In an interview for the *Dallas Morning News,* Dr. Lee

[1] Frank X. Tolbert, "Headliner Portrait."

commented that it took him almost a year to learn that Tennessee people didn't like jokes, no matter how gentle, in the pulpit. He remembered that once he commented on the action of a Methodist bishop who had resigned to give his full time to preaching. Three Methodist bishops and the ex-bishop, who had resigned, were sitting behind Dr. Lee as he spoke. "I said I didn't feel very comfortable commenting about this case hemmed in as I was by one resigned bishop and three unresigned bishops. And do you know no one laughed, except the unresigned bishops."

Two successful years at Vanderbilt established Lee's reputation as an educator as well as a scholar. The School of Religion was languishing when he arrived at Vanderbilt in 1936, but:

Dr. Lee's energetic interest, fine personality, broad contacts, and interest in the school and young ministers gave the school just what it needed to get back on its feet. The faculty and staff rallied behind his guidance at once. We began to get more and superior students. Everything took on new life. We grew rapidly in every phase, and gained the respect of the other departments.[2]

The young ministers in the School of Religion reacted to Dr. Lee with the same admiration and devotion as those in his homiletics class at Southern Methodist University. Mrs. Grace N. Teague, the librarian of the school, wrote:

Our daily chapel services lasted only a few minutes, but students and staff were loath to miss the nuggets of wisdom he would share with us. . . . Some of them I remember and repeat to this day. In the years that have followed I have observed the maneuvers designed to get students to come to chapel services, and think to myself, "Dr. Lee never had this problem." Is it, I wonder, because he had something to say?

[2] Comments by Elizabeth Albernathy, registrar.

In the spring of 1938, Ohio Wesleyan University of Delaware, Ohio, began the search for a new president. The selection committee there apparently had only one doubt about Umphrey Lee's qualifications and wrote to Elmer Scott, Executive Secretary of the Dallas Civic Foundation, asking specifically about Lee's technique as a money raiser. They wanted to know whether he was a man who shunned financial contacts and willingly pushed all plans for raising money off on committees, or a man who raised money through committees and showed wisdom in thus entrusting to laymen work they could do better than he. Elmer Scott's answer on this rather fine distinction must have been favorable in the eyes of the committee, for a second letter stated that they were trying to interest Dr. Lee in the position.[3]

While the family spent the summer vacationing in Red River, New Mexico, Dr. Lee considered the offer carefully and concluded that it was his duty to return to Vanderbilt. Both Umphrey, Jr. and Mary Lee were happy with his decision.

These years at Vanderbilt were memorable ones in Mary Lee's married life. Basically shy and frequently worried and depressed, she suffered agonizingly in the public role she had to play as the wife of a popular minister and, later, as the wife of a university president. This was known only to her family and closest friends, for her desire to help her husband was so great that, if a public appearance was inevitable, she forced herself to carry it off with great aplomb.

Mary Lee was a tall, stately woman with an attractive, even-featured face. Her public countenance was calm, poised, and friendly, and in her gayer moods she was attractively vivacious and entertaining. In this gay mood she would maintain that *things* were always happening to her, and she could make an amusing story about the time, on one of her early morning

[3] Letters to Elmer Scott from Ernest F. Amy, May 30, 1938 and June 9, 1938.

walks, when someone thought that she was a suspicious character and called the police; or an embarrassing episode at Neiman-Marcus in Dallas, where, as a nervous new mother-in-law, she was buying a dress for her new daughter-in-law. Because of a confusion in names or a breakdown in communication, her credit rating was challenged. In Mary Lee's humorous version, her interrogator asked if her husband was regularly employed and Mrs. Lee replied, "I *think* so. He has been president of Southern Methodist University for several years now!" Suitable apologies were made to Mrs. Lee the next day.

As she grew older and increasingly handicapped by diabetes, Mary Lee could be formidable. Her son tells of a time when she startled an audience at the Highland Park Methodist Church sometime in the 1950's. A visiting speaker had expostulated at some length about the changes made in the discipline, after the union in 1939 of the branches of the Methodist Church. The clergyman spoke quite disparagingly of archaic language, old forms, and the general clumsiness of old ceremonies. Mrs. Lee took this to be a criticism of Dr. Lee's preference for the more formal service and, possibly, resented the sneering at everything old. Always quick to act in defense of her husband, she restrained herself as long as she could and then rose, in all her dignity, faced the surprised speaker, and announced in a loud, clear voice, "After all, *God* is *old!*" and marched out of the church.

The years at Vanderbilt were relaxed ones for her. She did not feel great pressure as the wife of a dean. Dr. Lee expected to remain in Nashville and bought a house, a big, white, southern colonial type with a balcony across the front and white Corinthian columns. There were a spacious lawn, low stone walls, and stately trees. The house had been the property of an eccentric professor, and nine-year-old Umphrey, Jr. was entranced by the full-length mural of Captain Ahab chasing Moby Dick that covered the wall of one room, and he wished that they could keep the myriads of miniature railroad tracks, hills, stations, and control tower that were the remnants of the previous professor's hobby. The tracks had to go, but the mural remained when the room was converted into a study for Dr. Lee.

Umphrey, Jr., had grown out of the baby years when he had been addicted to running away. When he was smaller the Lees had made a harness and leather leash to fit him so that his cousin Elizabeth, who assisted in his care, could walk or shop without constant fear of losing her charge in the crowd. The big house on Jones Avenue (now Fairfax Avenue) in Nashville had Dutch doors, bay windows, and a secret panel leading to a secret room under the stairs that the curious little boy was fascinated to explore.

These were pleasant years and both Mary Lee and Umphrey, Jr. urged Dr. Lee to turn down offers that would take them away from Nashville. Mary Lee did not share her husband's passion for scholarship and research but in her attractively vivacious mood she was an entertaining companion and, then, "Umphrey Lee was happiest."

These comparatively quiet years at Vanderbilt University were possibly the most tranquil of Dr. Lee's adult life. There was gratification in his success in rebuilding and revitalizing the Vanderbilt School of Religion, but his greatest satisfaction was that he had time for teaching and research. By 1938, Lee had published his first seven most extensive books and had laid the foundation for those he would write later. Perusal of his sermons and writings would indicate that he had arrived at his philosophy of life and religion; his speaking style, which had something of the "shouter" in it in his younger preaching days, was taking on the forceful calm of later years.

"Glad *You* Could Be with *Us*"

On September 30, 1938, at the formal opening of the 1938-1939 year of the School of Religion of Vanderbilt University in the chapel of Wesley Hall, Dean Umphrey Lee gave the address, directed principally to the student ministers.[4]

The beliefs expressed in this speech synthesized much of his religious rhetoric. He dealt with the place or function of religion in an era of change; the growing emphasis on the secular, with a subsequent decline of religion's influence; the conflict between church and state; and the lack of religious emphasis in education. Woven throughout the fabric of most of Dr. Lee's sermons was the thread of the idea that the world's hope lay in the renovation of authentic religious understanding of human experience.

In developing this address, Dr. Lee observed that before 1900, moral cause and effect seemed fairly obvious. It had been a world of personal contact. People looked into the eyes of the men with whom they dealt. In business, the manager was the owner, not thousands of faceless stockholders. People were steeped in religious thought and phraseology. Religious teaching was commonplace in the schools; a chapel period was usual. The majority of the population was Protestant. Other religions were ignored. It was assumed that all in an audience were Protestants or ought to be. They "wrestled with ancient ethical problems and never heard of relativity."

Dean Lee emphasized how different the world of 1938 was from the world of 1900. As young preachers, his audience would upon graduation find themselves preaching to a generation that would have little knowledge of religion—in fact, one that had not thought about religion at all. "You are preparing to preach to a disillusioned world." He warned that one does not preach to the modern world by "stale

---

[4] "The Preacher and the Modern Mind." *School of Religion Notes: The School of Religion, Vanderbilt University.*

exhortation" alone. Not that the old copybook maxims were no longer as true as they were in a simpler world. Religion to be effective had to be related to the needs of a modern industrial society, "a society in which many felt that science could do what God couldn't." The young pastor would have to start from the beginning. He could not assume that the congregation believed in God. Furthermore, the modern pastor could belong to "no class and no interest; he alone stands on the Godward side of man. . . ." However, the "religious sanction, once powerful in the minds of men, cannot be invoked for a generation to whom there is no religious sanction."

Thorough preparation and dedication appeared to Dean Lee to be the answer. "There is no place for one who will not wrestle mightily. . . . We shall cut a sorry figure if we have nothing but certain frills of learning and tricks of the trade; it is a poor time for those who can only walk delicately like Agag, in a world of hard realities." With typical Lee humor, he observed: "Jesus said something about the small market for pearls among swine; but he did not think that thereby the pearls had lost their value; he only felt sorry for the hogs."

Mr. Decherd Turner, librarian of Bridwell Library at Southern Methodist University, in the late spring of 1958 drove Dr. and Mrs. Lee from Dallas to Wichita Falls, Texas, where Dr. Lee was to deliver the Perkins Lecture at the First Methodist Church. A discussion of simplicity in prayer arose and Dr. Lee commented, "I often feel the most meaningful and fundamental prayer is: 'Now I lay me down to sleep. If I should die before I wake, I pray the Lord my soul to take.' " There was a glow, a patina of peaceful resignation on his countenance as he repeated the childhood prayer. Dr. Lee died two months later. When one contemplates the childhood prayer held in such high regard by Dr. Lee, his statement from an address delivered twenty years earlier, that morning in Nashville in 1938, comes to mind: "We . . . have our own lonely way to tread."

Catholics, Dr. Lee felt, were in several respects more astute than Protestants in their understanding of psychology, communication, and sociology. First of all, Catholicism was on psychologically firmer ground in its premise that ceremony in the church service enhances the religious experience; there is a basic human need of ritual. The sights and sounds of childhood, even the smells which a child associates with religion, exert a strong emotional influence on the adult. Lee felt that Protestants might possibly learn from Catholics in this respect: "The Catholics have been wiser than the Protestants. They have seen to it that certain sensual accompaniments of worship greet the man wherever he goes. They have not under-rated man's carnality. Remember Browning's bishop who longed to 'feel the steady candle flame, and taste good, strong, thick, stupefying incense smoke'?"

He seemed to feel that Protestants might enhance their communication effectiveness if they emulated the Catholics who spoke with some unanimity—at least, more so than Protestants. Later in another lecture at Vanderbilt, he observed: "It is understandable that some Protestants would sigh for a voice in some ways comparable to the voice of Rome." His concern was evident when he noted that, "Protestantism has many voices but no single voice." He then went on to say that the Protestant wish to speak in a more unified voice will not be realized as long as: "Protestants regard their churches as they do, refusing to concede to the clergy or to any group the right to speak ex cathedra, or even with the blessings of the hierarchy." (*Render Unto the People,* pp. 122-24.)

In that same lecture, delivered in the mid 40's, he noted that the effectiveness of the Catholic Church was due in part to the fact that it ministered to "all sorts and conditions of men." There was some truth in the charge that many Protestant churches were frequently class societies. "No amount of wise social leadership will offset a ministry to one social or economic class."

VI

"Father Confessor, Friend, and Counselor to Us All"

As early as 1929, it had been surmised that Dr. Charles C. Selecman, president of Southern Methodist University, would be elevated to a bishopric when the General Conference of the Methodist Church South met in Dallas in May 1930. Dr. Horace M. Whaling, Jr., vice-president of SMU, and Dr. Umphrey Lee, then on leave at Columbia University, were prominently mentioned as successors. Nothing came of this although speculation and agitation continued.

Nine years later, in early 1938, there were persistent rumors that Dr. Charles C. Selecman's stormy tenure as president of SMU was about to end. The board of trustees of Southern Methodist University had shown remarkable prescience over the twenty-three years of the University's existence in their choice of men to head the young school. The first president, the reticent, precise, scholarly scientist Dr. Robert S. Hyer, had struggled to set a high educational tone and point the University on its respected course.

Dr. H. A. Boaz, later Bishop Boaz, was the money raiser without peer who was needed to keep SMU solvent through the lean years. Dr. Selecman was the strong administrator needed to enforce a measure of organization and control onto a distinguished, individualistic faculty of restless spirits. Now the time had come for change. The personal prestige of a scholar was essential, but a scholar with other attributes of leadership.

Some Dallas businessmen early decided that Umphrey Lee would be the needed man and wrote asking whether or not he would consider such an appointment were it offered. The already existing tension between Lee and President Selecman was not lessened when Selecman heard and misjudged Lee's passive part in the interchange.

In the spring of 1938, at the General Conference of the Methodist Church South in Birmingham, Dr. Selecman was elected to the episcopacy, and the search for a new president for Southern Methodist University began in earnest. Mr. Ezra S. Fudge, a wealthy leader of the North Texas Conference lay delegation to Birmingham and a member of the church's general board of finance, reported later that he had immediately asked Dr. Lee if he would consider coming to Southern Methodist University. "He looked at me a long time," said Mr. Fudge, "and then he said, 'Yes, Ezra, I'll come, but only under certain conditions.'" Mr. Fudge interpreted this to mean that Dr. Lee wanted to be a real president empowered to exercise a free hand. He felt strongly that Dr. Lee was the rare churchman who was also vitally interested in education and would not later leave the position to become a bishop.

After Dr. Selecman's retirement from the presidency, the board of trustees appointed a committee of seven under the chairmanship of Frank L. McNeny to select names for presentation to the whole board of trustees. Mr. McNeny seemed to favor a layman for the post, as did some other members, while Eugene McElvaney, vice president of the First National Bank in Dallas, and S. J. Hay, Jr., president of the Great National Life Insurance Co., circulated petitions asking for Dr. Lee. Mr. McElvaney presented these petitions to the board of trustees, making an appeal for the appointment of Dr. Lee.

Some thirty names were considered by the committee. Most prominently mentioned were Dr. J. N. Score of Fort Worth, Dr. Paul Quillian of Houston, Dr. W. M. Alexander of Nashville, Dr. Eugene B. Hawk of SMU, Dr. John T. Anderson of New York University, and Dr. Lee.

A number of those suggested for the position were invited to appear before the nominating committee. Several did come for interviews with the Board, the faculty committee, and representatives of the ex-students association. Dr. Lee was invited but did not accept.

It was consistent with Dr. Lee's character for him to play a passive role. He was not certain that he wanted heavier administrative duties than the deanship at Vanderbilt entailed. The development of the school there was just beginning to reward his efforts. Mrs. Lee and Umphrey, Jr. were happy in Nashville and did not want to leave. The presidency of Southern Methodist University could be a stepping stone to a bishopric but, as has been stated before, his friends believed that he had no ambition to be a bishop. Although Dr. Lee knew of all the efforts in his behalf, he was not sure that he wanted them to succeed. If, through no effort of his own, the position was offered, he would feel that it was right for him to accept. As he viewed himself, any gesture, even that of appearing before the committee, would constitute bustling aggressiveness.

Three hundred Dallas businessmen signed the petition asking for Dr. Lee. Students and ex-students made requests of the Board. Equally active on his behalf were Leonard T. Blaisdell, an executive of the General Electric Company, Bryce Twitty, Superintendent of Baylor Hospital and former president of the ex-students association, and J. Roscoe Golden, a prominent Dallas attorney.

The committee of the board of trustees began its series of interviews and investigations. The list was soon reported to have narrowed to seven and, finally, to four. The one strong contender who was not a clergyman was Dr. John T. Anderson who had an established reputation as an educator.

Excitement mounted in Dallas and at Southern Methodist University when, in early November, the committee of seven met to make a final choice for recommendation to the board of trustees. The greatest secrecy was maintained as the committee gathered in dignified silence for a meeting in the vacated president's office.

The excitement was felt by Mrs. Loretta Hawkins, the secretary to the president. She scanned each face hopefully as they gave her a restrained greeting. What was to be the final meeting dragged on. Finally one of the committee members, Bishop A. Frank Smith, chairman of the board of trustees, came out of the committee-room door, closed it softly and asked solemnly where he could find a telephone for a private conversation. Mrs. Hawkins directed him. After a time he returned, thanked her solemnly again and rejoined the others behind that mysterious door. Mrs. Hawkins could no longer concentrate on her work but was resigned to waiting when her telephone rang and the operator said, "Could you tell me who just made that call to Dean Umphrey Lee in Nashville, Tennessee? "

Umphrey Lee was named the fourth president of Southern Methodist University on November 7, 1938, by unanimous vote of the board of trustees. He was to assume his new duties January 19, 1939, at the beginning of the second semester. Expressions of approval came from citizens, faculty, and students. Tom Grimes, president of the SMU Student's Association, wrote in *The Campus*, "We feel he is understanding as well as able. We know he is liberally inclined. Perhaps his coming will bring that long-contended question of dancing on the campus to a head."

When the newspapers in Nashville carried the announcement that Dean Lee was leaving Vanderbilt, it was "Black Monday" to everyone. Students lined up at his office to say that they were transferring to Perkins School of Theology at

Southern Methodist University, and Mrs. Grace N. Teague, the librarian, wore a black dress as a symbol of her distress. She has said that he was "father confessor, friend, and counselor to us all."

Unwilling to wait for Dr. Lee until January, the Dallas Chamber of Commerce asked him to come from Nashville to address their next meeting a few days later. A calm, widely smiling Umphrey Lee arrived at Union Station and stepped from the train that morning into a large and happy group of newspapermen, cameramen, University officials, and friends. He was the houseguest of Mr. and Mrs. Eugene McElvaney.

Only twenty days before this, Britain, France, and Italy, at a parley in Munich, had agreed to Germany's dismemberment of Czechoslovakia, and Chamberlain had returned to London with his message of "peace in our time." Dr. Lee had long been a student of the European political situation, and he felt that even those not fond of reading the omens should sense the danger in the allied capitulation. In his address at the Adolphus Hotel before 1,400 diners, he warned all to steer a midway course between jitters and careless complacency or be in danger of losing our civilization.

At once SMU made plans to welcome the Lees in January. S. J. Hay, Jr. was appointed chairman of a committee of ex-students to arrange a "huge" banquet honoring Lee; he indicated that they would provide "a good old country-town welcome." Then postponements began. It proved to be impossible to vacate the office of dean of the School of Religion at Vanderbilt without more preparation. Dr. Lee was supposed to arrive the first of February, and he did come to attend the meeting of the board of trustees and to accept, formally, the enlarged and refurbished J. J. Perkins Hall of Administration at the dedication ceremonies.

He inspected and admired the furnishings, the gift of a committee of Dallas businessmen as a personal tribute to

Dr. Lee. He was "full of plans and visions" for the University and parried questions of reporters about SMU's burning student protest issue—the ban on holding dances on the campus: "I would prefer not to discuss the matter of dancing on the campus until I have to." [1] He returned to Nashville, and on February 8, *The Campus* carried the notice that Dr. Lee would "take over" later since the delay in obtaining his release had already kept him from opening the new semester.

The next headline said, "Lee to take over March 1," but March 1 arrived and Dr. Lee did not. Word ran around the campus that no message had come from him. The evening issue of the *Dallas Times Herald* read "Whereabouts Unknown" and reported that all was bedlam in the president's office as the harassed secretaries tried to answer telephone calls, telegrams, and personal inquiries. Since the new president had said that he "wanted to come into office without any fuss," they had, all day, expected him to walk in any minute.

The next day Dr. and Mrs. Lee with Umphrey, Jr. and his dog Bozo arrived in the family Pontiac several hours ahead of their furniture. Mrs. Lee had not been well, and they had spent the night fifty miles away in Greenville, Texas, so that they could be rested and fresh when they reached Dallas. Thursday night the family was at the Stoneleigh Hotel, and Friday they established residence with their furniture and large collection of books in the remodeled presidential home on Hillcrest Avenue.

President Umphrey Lee assumed his duties on March 2. His first act was to dictate a letter of appreciation to Bishop Selecman for his telegram of good wishes. Four days later, 300 members of the University community met the three Lees at a reception in Perkins Hall, without speeches. The student

[1] *Dallas Morning News*, February 7, 1939.

body planned a "torch parade" on Monday night after fraternity and sorority meetings. They were to gather at the gymnasium and, led by the band, march to the steps of Dallas Hall for welcoming speeches. But they were persuaded that the pace had been too strenuous for the Lees the previous weeks, and the students regretfully called off the procession. The following Tuesday night Dr. Lee addressed the Methodist laymen of the Dallas district, his first public address after assuming the presidency.

Great changes had taken place since Umphrey Lee was one of 706 students who enrolled in Southern Methodist University in 1915. He now headed a teaching staff of 125; an enrollment of 2,512, one out of ten of whom were from outside Texas; and a plant worth more than $6,000,000. But greater changes were to come in the next few years.

All spring and summer a feeling of uncertainty had dominated the SMU campus. Bishop Selecman had retired from the presidency as soon as he became bishop, and Dean Eugene Blake Hawk had assumed authority as interim president until the election of a permanent president. When the University opened its fall semester of 1938, a new president had not yet been selected and a feeling of melancholy descended on the campus.

The first faculty meeting of the fall semester was a disheartening affair. Dean Hawk painted a gloomy picture of the University's financial situation and indicated that there might not be enough money to pay faculty salaries in full for the year. Layton Bailey, business manager of SMU, presented a discouraging budget. Even older faculty members, who had been through SMU's depression, left the meeting crestfallen, and new faculty members were convinced that they should never have come to Southern Methodist University. As soon as the acceptance of Umphrey Lee was made public in November, there was a noticeable change in attitude on the campus. A few note of cheer and confidence was felt.

When Dr. Lee finally arrived, the whole campus was exuberant. There was no more talk of doubtful salary payments. Although that first year there was a deficit of nearly $200,000 (tuition vs. amount spent) the money for salaries was found somewhere and, whatever agony and uncertainty was involved, the faculty generally was not burdened with it. The president inaugurated a Sustentation Fund drive, and Dallas businessmen came to expect the annual visit of SMU's perennial money raiser, Bishop Boaz, joined later by economist Dr. Arthur A. Smith.

The presence of Umphrey Lee in the president's office and on the campus acted as a tonic on faculty and students. The gentle, captivating grin that puffed out his plump cheeks, lighting up his whole face, and his unique ability to remember names and faces immediately endeared Umphrey Lee to those who had not known him before. He possessed an undeniable calm friendliness that delighted students, scholars, businessmen, and sportsmen alike.

Dr. Lee's personal prestige was immense and did not lessen in all the years of his presidency. If he failed to solve a problem or made a poor decision, his indulgent friends and associates would assume that, either the problem was insoluble, someone had given him the wrong advice, or he had decided thus because of his reluctance to hurt someone involved.

Associates express evaluation of President Lee in different ways: "There was something about him that reached out to you. When he came through the outer office each morning and spoke to the girls, their day was made. . . . He was thoughtful and considerate of those under him. He could live with their shortcomings. . . . He never made anyone his scapegoat, and he assumed full responsibility for the actions of his staff and faculty. He always gave anyone connected with his administration credit for achievement, and he never assumed credit for the work done under him" (Hemphill Hosford). "He was a just person" (Loretta Hawkins). "He didn't meddle in the details of running your department" (James Stewart). "He had a way of giving advice so that a person thought he had worked it out for himself—and felt very intelligent" (Rose Malone Lee). "I didn't work for Umphrey Lee; we worked together—as partners. He had the ability to make his department heads feel that he thought they had enough sense to run their departments" (Stanley Patterson).

The humorous was rarely missing. Stanley Patterson, superintendent of Buildings and Grounds, remembers that Dr. Lee received a letter from some lady praising Mr. Patterson for some kindness he had shown her on the campus. Dr. Lee forwarded the letter to "Mr. Pat" with an attached note: "I'll thank you not to take credit around here. If any credit is flying around, I'll take it. You just go on and work!"

Dr. Lee was meticulous about appreciation. Fifty-eight "thank you" letters went out to faculty members and their wives who had assisted at an SMU open house welcoming the members of the Texas Congress of Parents and Teachers in November 1940. Fifteen days after Dr. Lee assumed the presidency, letters were sent to all Methodist ministers in what he considered to be SMU's territory, asking for support and assistance. He particularly wanted names and information about promising students due to graduate from local high schools.

One of his first actions was to set up nine faculty self-study committees. He hoped to use that great developer, responsibility, to get the faculty busy and involved in university evaluation and perspective. Foremost on the agenda were plans to increase the academic prestige of Southern Methodist University.

There was no period of tranquillity after Dr. Lee arrived

at SMU. Scarcely was he established in his chair in the office of the president when the ominous sounds of approaching war in Europe grew louder. In the spring of 1938, Germany had occupied Austria, and on September 29-30, 1938, came the infamously memorable days of Munich. Thirteen days after Lee arrived at his new offices, on March 2, 1939, Germany seized Czechoslovakia, and exactly five months after that March 2 morning, Germany invaded Poland and World War II began. All the new president's addresses to students contained some reference to the growing tensions, combined with gratitude that the young people at SMU were going to school and not to war. At one important Forum meeting Dr. Lee led a discussion on "Foreign Propaganda Methods Soon to Be Experienced by Americans."

The fall of 1939, Lee's first full semester, was an eventful one and flung him quickly into the mainstream of university life. Southern Methodist University was beginning its silver anniversary year, and Homecoming was planned as a double celebration with the president's formal inauguration early in November. The Lees attended the Pigskin Review on the night of November 3. There were pep rallies, contests, a parade, a barbecue, a sing-song, a band concert, and the first Student Council sponsored dance on the campus, topped off with the big football game, SMU vs. Texas University, when Coach Matty Bell's team beat Texas by a score of 10-0 before a crowd of 23,000 in Ownby Stadium.

On Sunday the gala weekend took a more serious turn, as described before, with the religious convocation. The four-day series of festivities reached its climax with the inauguration of Umphrey Lee as the fourth president of the University and ended with the evening reception honoring the new president and Mrs. Lee.

Dr. Lee had already announced many of his plans for SMU. His effect on the University had been immediate. He had enlarged the faculty, increased the health service, launched a building program, inaugurated a student employment and placement service. He had broached the subject of a foreign student exchange, possibly with a German university. World War II began before the program could be implemented. Somehow Dr. Lee even found time to speak at a gigantic pep rally before the football game with Baylor University, and the next day saw his team win by a score of 21-0. Frank X. Tolbert once described the scene in President Lee's office: "Members of Dr. Lee's staff were coming in and out. The big, smiling university president signed his name to papers as he talked. Yet there was a calm, relaxed atmosphere in the office. There has been a calm, relaxed atmosphere at SMU ever since Umphrey Lee became president in 1939."

VII

"War Has Never Ended War"—1940-1946

By the fall of 1940, Southern Methodist University students were personally and emotionally involved in the war in Europe. A few students set off for Canada and the Royal Air Force. It had been announced in August that SMU was to train civilian pilots and that defense training courses were to be set up in the school of engineering. The programs began almost at once, and both were functioning by December, with the cost borne by the government.

In the fall, Dr. Lee's first message to the students concerned the National Defense program, still in a formative stage. The University instituted a plan enabling students to complete requirements for the Bachelor's degree in three years, before the draft age of twenty-one. Four hundred and six faculty and undergraduate men between the ages of twenty-one and thirty-six registered for the draft in October. Campus interest in politics was also high, and in a campus poll Roosevelt led Willkie for president of the United States 57.6 percent to 42.4 percent.

The president's attention was also directed to many other problems on campus. In November 1940, Ownby Stadium's south end bleachers collapsed during a Saturday football game, injuring thirty-six of the 2,500 spectators. Dr. Lee spent Sunday at the hospital with the seven victims who were still hospitalized.

In December, students and faculty, including President Lee, signed a petition to create a committee of 100 to urge Texas representatives in Congress to support unlimited aid to Great

Britain, and the campus community became increasingly agitated over totalitarianism.

The war effort did not absorb all of Dr. Lee's time or energies. In 1940, the first Institute of the National Congress of Christians and Jews to be held in the Southwest was conducted at Southern Methodist University under the sponsorship of Dr. Lee, President Homer P. Rainey of the University of Texas, and United States Senator Morris Sheppard. Dr. Lee's old friend of Trinity days, Hastings Harrison, was the Southwest Director of the NCCJ.

Dr. Lee was interested in planning a new alumni participation and gift program. The president's report to the board of trustees listed twelve buildings which would ultimately be needed by the University, and suggested that a special committee should set up a program of buildings, funds, and endowment needs.

The North Texas Conference of the Methodist Church shared Dr. Lee's attention. In March he was in Columbus, Ohio for an important committee meeting. In April he attended the General Conference, and in October the North Texas Conference met in Greenville, Texas. There he gave the memorial address for the ministers who had died during the year, and he was active in promoting a scholarship plan to erase the $30,000 deficit facing the School of Theology at SMU.

During his first year at SMU, Dr. Lee was instrumental in founding the Community Course in cooperation with Temple Emanu-El; thirty years later, it is still one of Dallas' most popular series of cultural events. On the campus he established the SMU Bureau of Student Opinion and followed with interest a long and heated campus agitation for courses in social hygiene, as *The Campus* delicately phrased sex education. He watched the work progress on the $458,000 Fondren Library, gift of Mr. and Mrs. W. W. Fondren. It was to be dedicated in January.

While Dr. Lee was attempting to keep SMU solvent and the teachers employed, he was also active in the war effort in many other ways. He had plugged aid to Britain as national peace insurance during half-time activities at the New Year's Day Cotton Bowl game between the Texas Aggies and Fordham University on January 1, 1941. Forty thousand people in the Cotton Bowl and a vast national radio audience heard Kate Smith sing "God Bless America," and Dr. Lee plead, "But if the democracies lose in Europe, we shall not go home to take up in peace once more our struggle for a better life for our children. We shall go back to a raw and brutal world with only a faint hope that maybe sometime our children's children may crawl back through blood and tears to the liberties we now enjoy." [1]

A Reserve Officers training corps was established in January 1941, and a "Y" panel began debating United States intervention in the war. In February, thirty-three SMU students were called for the draft but were deferred until June. Dr. Lee urged students to stay in college until the government decided otherwise, but there was a rush to enlist.

The same year a new School of Business was created at Southern Methodist University, and Dr. Lee was elected president of the Association of Schools and Colleges of the Methodist Church at a conference in Pasadena, California. Later he attended a National Defense Conference in Baltimore.

The exigencies of the moment removed first priority from academic achievement to University survival. No small problem was the financial situation. Wartime erosion of the student body was somewhat balanced by the Navy V 12 program and the War Industries Training program. Faculty members who no longer were needed in the regular schedule were pressed

[1] *Dallas Morning News,* January 2, 1941.

into teaching in the defense programs. Southern Methodist's expenses during Dr. Lee's first fiscal year totaled $742,000 while only $557,000 came in from tuition and fees. Money had to be raised for current expenses, and Dr. Lee also started searching for a way to get a Student Center building, which he considered of first priority.

But Pearl Harbor, December 7, 1941, brought the United States actively into the war and non-war needs had to be postponed. To the students at SMU the news of Pearl Harbor came as something fantastic and incredible. The time for discussion was ended; they knew they were involved in a war they must win. On the wave of the first reaction, the SMU School of Music decided the day after Pearl Harbor to cancel their performance of "Madame Butterfly." Someone said, "Pinkerton is such an unspeakable cad!"

After the Pearl Harbor catastrophe, the pace for SMU and for Dr. Lee accelerated. He was the principal speaker at a mass meeting at Fair Park in Dallas to crystallize public opinion and impress the leaders in Washington that the nation should be put on an all-out war basis in 1942. At this "WE WANT ACTION" meeting Lee pointed out that the country was not equipped mentally or economically for a war that might determine our very existence.

In May, Dr. Lee found time to be present to be honored with a Doctor of Law at Ohio Wesleyan University, citing him as a "gracious Christian gentleman of the South, careful student of John Wesley, civic leader, capable lecturer, effective preacher of the Word, author, president of a great sister university." He had received a D. Litt. from Southwestern University in Georgetown, Texas, two years previously.

During the four years after Pearl Harbor, Dallas life was dominated by the war. In the fall of 1943, SMU was offering fifty-eight courses to 1,094 students in the engineering, science, and management training program established in 1940 to help train personnel for war plants in Dallas and twenty other Texas cities. Thirteen thousand men and women had already gone through some 536 of these classes. SMU had changed from the semester to the quarter plan and finally changed again to a trimester plan. Correspondence courses were offered to men in the service, and more students left to enter the armed services.

Dr. Lee was appointed state chairman for Texas of the United Service Organization (USO) and, in addition, began in 1943 a series as commentator over radio station KRLD in Dallas on "Present and Post-War Conditions." By nature a man who recoiled from any violence or brutality, he had lived through one world war and the so-called peace between the wars. In 1925, Dr. Lee, the historian, had ironically stated his opinion of the slogan "war to end wars," of isolationism and pacifism:

The war [World War I] has not ended war. There has hardly been a day since the Armistice was signed in 1918 when there has not been war: the Sinn–Fein rebellion; the Russian revolution; the Greco-Turkish war. The war to end war, which was "ended" in 1918, has been continued or reflected in all the years since then.

Not only did the war not end war, but it made future war almost inevitable. As we look back now, it seems that we must have been childishly optimistic to have believed that out of the war could come a united world. (*Jesus the Pioneer*, p. 54.)

In commenting on post-War I isolationism he said, "America has withdrawn into her impossible policy of isolation." He continued, using his characteristic technique of reiteration of a thematic phrase:

The Great War [WWI] did not end war. It made the world about as safe as a gasoline tank around which children play with matches.

"War Has Never Ended War"—1940-1946

As a matter of fact, war has never ended war, nor has it done any other constructive thing. We said a good many silly things during the war about men finding their souls in battle. (*Jesus the Pioneer,* p. 56.)

Dr. Lee presented a paradox. He rejected war as a method of settling international disputes, but he stated, "Personally, I have not been able to subscribe to any consistent pacifist program." (*Jesus the Pioneer,* p. 57.) In 1943, during the second World War, he explored the age-old dilemma of Christian ethics: Can a Christian ethically or historically justify war? He answers in the affirmative, after exploring the questions in his book, *The Historic Church and Modern Pacificism.*

In this book, Dr. Lee theorizes that the nations of the world are at the stage of development that "pioneer communities of America were when the six-shooter was the only law." He asserts that "justice, relative as it always is, must be maintained between nations by force." Furthermore, international force of arms has "an ancient and honorable lineage." His authorities for this conclusion are: Saint Paul in Romans 13: 1-7; Augustine, who believed that "wars may be necessary to maintain order between nations," and "it is not impossible for one to please God while engaged in active military service"; Thomas Aquinas, "one of the great synthesizing minds of the Western world," who believed in "just wars"; Martin Luther; John Calvin; and John Wesley, who also did not "appear to have doubted the right of the Christian to fight." (Pp. 170-75.)

Dr. Lee was deeply involved in World War II. His own son was in training as a paratrooper, and casualty lists were carrying the names of many SMU ex-students killed in military service. The SMU losses eventually climbed to more than one hundred. Lee's radio addresses, that continued from August 1943, until June 1944, were broadcast each Friday evening and

107

published in full in the *Dallas Times Herald* the following Sunday.

Alarmed by the growing impatience of the American people and mounting criticism of the conduct of the war, Dr. Lee began his series of broadcasts by emphasizing that patience with the progress of the war and faith in our leaders were essential for success. He warned that unwise political pressures might override military decisions and lead to disaster. He repeated that we must put our faith in the generals and governmental leaders. To inform the public fully on every move would be also to inform the enemy.

Umphrey Lee was too wise and well-informed to believe in the infallibility of the military, but he was a realist and recognized that in the claims and dangers of the war situation there was no choice but to put aside skepticism and support those in command. The war period was no time for suspicious patriotism.

At this time, September 1943, there was worry that Stalin might pull Russia out of the war, yet the American people were complaining about the shortages of consumer goods and the drawing-out of the conflict. Speaking in specific terms, Dr. Lee pleaded: "Complain to the right people; don't talk loosely; don't give aid and comfort to the enemy by saying that if such and such thing doesn't happen there will be a revolution in this country."

He moved on to the problems that would arise as soon as the war was won. "We must prepare for peace as we prepare for war. . . . Whatever we do and whatever we desire, our future is tied up with the futures of other nations and peoples." [2] He advocated: sane thinking about the treatment of defeated nations; recognition of justice for all races, pointing out the preponderance of non-whites in the world; resistance to after-the-war relaxation and disillusionment that

[2] *Dallas Times Herald,* August 29, 1943.

108

would undermine our recognition of intangible values, our faith in democracy, and our appreciation of our fundamental freedoms.

In a radio address in March of 1944, he justified his support of the war and the bombing of Germany:

War is the denial of all that religious men and women hold dear, but—war is not merely the product of a series of stupid acts. These contribute, and we have done our share. But the war in this modern world is also brought on by the deliberate attempt of men who would dominate the world with their own particular type of despotism. And these have the chief sin of laying this terrible burden upon us. . . .

But there are times when men must recognize that they live in an evil world and that some would bind upon our children burdens heavier than men should bear. There are times when it seems to many of us that we must accept the terrible alternative and attempt to protect the little of civilization that man has so painfully evolved. . . .

I do not believe that this means that we must accept such a cruelty as the meaningless bombing of open cities but I do not see that we can choose death for millions of our sons to avoid the possibility of damage to innocent civilians.

Umphrey Lee was adroit in adapting himself to any audience or speaking situation. He never deviated from his point or his principles, but his skill was such that he left his audience in a spirit of agreement. However, he felt in retrospect that during the war, in his eagerness to be of service, he had violated his own rule and had gone before groups he did not understand and to whom he could not conform. One particular incident that had far-reaching disastrous results was the "WE WANT ACTION" meeting in 1942, mentioned previously.

At this time, little more than a year after the entry of the

United States into the conflict, war industries were pushing hard for full production. Unfortunately, Americans were not all unselfishly united in the war effort. Industrialists, laboring groups, and farmers each felt that the others were trying to benefit themselves first and serve the country second. One of the targets was the 40-hour work week and the time-and-a-half pay for overtime. An attempt was made, unsuccessfully, to persuade the Congress to extend the work week.

In Dallas, the idea for some organized demonstration was apparently touched off at a meeting of the Dallas Real Estate Board in February when the farmers and labor were accused of trying to make a profit out of the war and the meeting was given some publicity in the newspapers. Plans were soon made by a group of Dallas businessmen for a gigantic rally to be held at Fair Park Auditorium in March. Newspapers carried editorials, the Gold Star Mothers and citizen's groups were activated to arouse patriotic fervor. Letters to the editor flowed in, and large numbers of them were published. Most blamed labor for America's lack of preparedness and were violently anti-Roosevelt. A few put the blame on big business.

On the day before the rally the newspapers assured readers that the Sunday meeting was not meant as an attack on labor and quoted Karl Hoblitzelle, who headed the rally committee, that the sole purpose "is to bring about total war production . . . and to the further end that the duration of this war might be shortened and our boys brought home." [3]

The Sunday rally reached the pinnacle of patriotic demonstrations. Flags and bunting draped the auditorium. At the back of the stage was a large American flag and below it a large sign which read "Let's Start Winning the War." Parents of fighting men were honored guests, and mothers were presented corsages. Disabled veterans were seated on the stage.

---

[3] *Dallas Morning News,* March 21, 1942.

The Adamson and North Dallas High School bands played stirring marches outside. A public address system carried the program to those who could not get seats in the packed auditorium. There were patriotic songs sung by the audience and a Presentation of the Colors. The Oath of Allegiance was followed by numbers from the combined Dallas Male Chorus and the East Dallas Christian Church Chorus. At the end of the program the audience sang the "Star Spangled Banner," and the SMU band played until the crowd had left the auditorium.

After the speeches, copies of a proposed resolution were passed out to the audience and read by Mr. Hoblitzelle. The resolution called for prohibiting all lockouts, strikes, and excessive war profits; a 48-hour week; greater contribution by labor to the war effort; the closing of congressional doors to lobbyists slowing down the war effort; the uniting of our people. It was adopted by a rising vote of the audience.

When the motion was presented, a man near the rear of the hall tried to speak in protest. After the motion carried, another man near the front tried to gain recognition unsuccessfully.

These were two young economics professors from the University of Texas, and the newspapers published the story. This started a chain of events that led to the dismissal of the two young men and a confrontation between the board of regents and the president of the University of Texas, Homer P. Rainey, who resigned and later made an unsuccessful race for governor of the state.

Dr. Lee was not comfortable in an emotion-charged atmosphere. He later described the incident to his son, explaining that he had hesitated when asked to be the principal speaker at the rally. He knew, he said, that part of the motives were selfish, but he also believed that the avoidance of strikes was essential to assure war materials in sufficient quantity to win

111

the war. After much inner conflict, he became convinced that it was his patriotic duty to do all that he could.

His address that day was probably a disappointment to some. His calm remarks were not in accordance with the fighting mood of much of the audience. He called for "a moratorium on politics" and made a plea for some settlement of issues impeding the war effort.

Another incident during the war years, very disturbing to Dr. Lee, happened in 1944. For a time Umphrey Lee became the innocent central figure in a well-publicized national election scandal. Wendell L. Willkie was a strong contender for the Republican presidential nomination, and in 1943 an anti-Willkie book entitled *One Man-Wendell Willkie,* really a king-sized pamphlet, was published. It was written by C. Nelson Sparks, a former mayor of Akron, Ohio, where Willkie once practiced law. In the book were quotes from a letter supposedly signed by Harry Hopkins and written to Dr. Lee:

> Dear Humphrey,
>   What has been done with the . . . matter? Will you write me please? What developments in the other situation? Willkie is going to be the man, in my opinion, and I can promise you good cooperation from that quarter if you think it would be helpful? [4]

The general interpretation of the enigmatic letter was that Willkie was almost certain to be the Republican nominee for president of the United States and that the Democratic administration was willing to support Dr. Lee for the senate against Senator Tom Connally, Texas Democrat. The blotted-out word was thought by some to be "Alamo," a code word referring to the so-called conspiracy.[5]

[4] *The New York Times,* December 4, 1943.
[5] *Dallas Times Herald,* January 21, 1944.

Dr. Lee stated that he knew nothing about any letter or any conspiracy. Harry Hopkins branded the letter a forgery and asked for an FBI inquiry. It was noted from the beginning that, although the letter was couched in familiar terms, the writer did not know that Umphrey is not spelled with an H.

The so-called "Hopkins" letter became a *cause célèbre*, and there were charges and countercharges bringing in George M. Briggs, aide to Interior Secretary Ickes, Ickes himself, and Frank Phillips, Oklahoma oil man, who was supposed to have the original of the letter. There followed a grand jury investigation and Dr. Lee was subpoenaed.

Dallas papers carried the news as events developed. Mrs. Lee and a puzzled Dr. Lee left on January 9, 1944, to go to Washington by train. Dr. Lee assured the reporters that he did not even know Harry Hopkins.

In Washington, the Lees were guests of Assistant Attorney General Thomas C. Clark (later Justice of the Supreme Court). They were luncheon guests of Speaker Sam Rayburn and were entertained by several members of the Texas delegation. Harry Hopkins was in the hospital with one of his frequent attacks of illness, and Dr. Lee still did not meet him.

When Dr. Lee was testifying before the grand jury, he was asked his occupation. He replied that he was a Methodist minister. The interrogator then asked, "Then what the hell are you doing around here?" To which Dr. Lee replied, "That's what I'd like to know." After the ordeal the Lees relaxed with a pleasant sight-seeing vacation in the eastern states.

Briggs was indicted for forgery and mail fraud. Later he committed suicide, and others in the case were cleared. Dr. Lee may have been approached as a possible candidate to oppose Senator Connally, but all the events of his life would indicate how removed he was from desiring this sort of political image.

Dr. Lee's ordeal over the "Hopkins Letter" furnished the Dallas Bonehead Club entertainment at the club's first luncheon meeting after his return from Washington. The Bonehead Club, organized in 1920, is a group of fifty-seven fun-loving, prominent Dallas men who meet regularly and never miss an opportunity to inject the whimsical or waggish into the current scene. The "57" came originally from Heinz Varieties. The *Dallas Times Herald* of February 4, 1944, carried the following story:

Hopkins-Lee Case Taken Up by Boneheads, Pigeon Quizzed, "Letter" Found

"This is Dr. Umphrey Lee, president of Southern Methodist University, on my right," explained Gus Thomasson at the Friday luncheon meeting of the Bonehead Club in the Baker Hotel. "Will those who know or have heard of this man, please raise their hands?"

Out of the 57 members seated at the groups of tables, only five hands were slowly raised.

"It would seem, Dr. Lee, that there is some difficulty in establishing your identity even in your home town," Thomasson continued, and he explained that an unofficial investigation was being undertaken of the now famous alleged Hopkins-Lee letter. Thomasson then turned to a large bird cage on the speaker's table, which housed an unperturbed carrier pigeon.

Addressing the pigeon, Thomasson, in his best district-attorney manner, queried, "What is your name?" "My name is Alamo," answered the pigeon. When the pigeon answered, all members of the club sat forward on their chairs and looked about the nearby tables for the ventriloquist who, being a professional, escaped discovery.

"Did you, or did you not, deliver a certain letter to Dr. Lee?" The pigeon coldly regarded Thomasson for a moment, then replied calmly, "I did." "That is all. Will J. Howard Payne, postmaster, take the stand?" A search for Payne was made and a letter addressed to Dr. Lee and marked "personal" was found in one of Payne's pockets.

Prosecutor Thomasson fired, "This letter is old—why haven't you delivered it?"

Payne deliberated a moment, then replied, "Well, it's marked 'personal,' isn't it? Any letters marked that way have to be delivered by me personally, and I just can't seem to get around to all of them on time."

A little more than a year later the war ended. Germany surrendered May 7, 1945, and on August 14, Japan's surrender ended the war in the East, releasing veterans from both theaters of war. In September 1945, Southern Methodist University's enrollment was only 1,256, but by registration time for the winter trimester, veterans had started back to college and enrollment more than doubled to reach 2,600. The swollen enrollment, which in September of 1946 reached 6,534, 60 percent veterans, required more professors, more classroom space, and brought vexatious psychological problems with some returning veterans.

War surplus helped the University with 108 Trailorville housing units for veterans and their families; prefabs became cold and drafty classrooms and temporary faculty family housing. The Federal Works Agency even supplied a war surplus student center, large in size, if unattractive in decor.

The Aviation Training program had been fazed out in 1944, and in June of 1946, the Navy units left the campus, and the war was officially over for Southern Methodist University. New faculty members were recruited from everywhere and the University, under Dr. Lee's guidance, made the best of the situation until the enrollment stabilized and new permanent buildings could provide more adequate space. In February, during Minister's Week, Mrs. W. W. Fondren had announced the gift of $1,000,000 for a needed science building.

During the 1945-1946 school year three persons joined the University who were to have a close association with the president's office for many years. Dr. Willis M. Tate, an all-conference tackle on SMU's 1931 Southwest Conference championship football team and an outstanding sociology major who had received both his B.A. and M.A. degrees from Southern Methodist University, was executive assistant to the pastor of the First Methodist Church in Houston, Texas, Dr. Paul W. Quillian. He was asked to come to SMU as assistant dean of students in 1945. Less than three years later he was made dean of students; in two more years, vice president; and, at age forty-four, was selected to be the fifth president of Southern Methodist University.

Dr. Hemphill M. Hosford, 1919 graduate of SMU, who was then vice president of the University of Arkansas, was brought back to SMU as dean of the University and dean of the Faculty of Arts and Science in 1946, and, later, became vice president and provost until his retirement.

The third additon to the staff, in close association with the president, was Rose Malone, a new secretary in the president's office who later did much of Dr. Lee's private work, typed his speeches and his book, *Render Unto the People,* and continued in a more personal relationship as she was married to Umphrey Lee, Jr. in 1953.

Administrators and members of the office staff who worked closely with Dr. Lee recognized him as a man of quality deserving respect and loyalty. They also recognized that his discernible vulnerable spot as an administrator was his reluctance to say "no," or take positive action that he felt would hurt someone. His staff members and administrative associates developed a protective attitude and were quick to come to his defense or assistance, particularly when they felt that someone was taking advantage of him. They tried to erect a shield to protect him from their group as well as from outsiders.

Rose Malone Lee remembers two examples of this protective attitude when the office staff feared that Dr. Lee's reputation was in jeopardy. Once in a while Dr. Lee had lunch downtown at the Golden Pheasant restaurant. For many years the Golden Pheasant, renowned for its good food, was a meeting place for a group interested in helping alcoholics. As a new secretary, Rose Malone told a caller that Dr. Lee was at the Golden Pheasant because he was a member of Alcoholics Anonymous. The whole office staff converged on her, and a hasty correction was made.

After SMU's graduating classes became so large that Dr. Lee found it impossible to sign each diploma personally, the president's office staff resorted to a projector machine to sign a duplicate of Dr. Lee's signature. This equipment was kept confidentially in the office, for it was felt that students enjoyed feeling that their diplomas had been signed personally by Dr. Lee. One day someone asked a new girl in the office where Rose Malone was. She replied that Rose was in the conference room signing Dr. Lee's signature to the diplomas. "The office staff reacted as if a bomb had exploded."

A strong feeling of camaraderie always existed in the president's office. There was a kitchenette off the office, where Dr. Lee and Dr. Hosford often joined the staff for morning coffee. Sometimes Mrs. Lee and Mrs. Hosford would help celebrate someone's birthday. The atmosphere was relaxed, but "there was a certain formality that no one ever overstepped."

Rose Malone Lee's evaluation of Dr. Lee, as viewed from a secretary's desk, is echoed by Elizabeth Abernathy who was his secretary during his years at Vanderbilt. She reflects: "Working with him was not only a liberal education but a delightful experience. He liked to watch me take, in shorthand, his dictation. The little characters fascinated him. Sometimes, in the midst of dictating, he would suddenly go off on some other line of thought, and watch me perk up and give him a quizzical look! He was always kind, helpful, considerate and appreciative."

Southern Methodist University's yearbook, the *Rotunda,* was dedicated to Dr. Lee in 1945:

> "I hold the world but as a stage
> A stage where every man must play a part."

It is not often our privilege to see enacted on that stage a role as great as that played by SMU's president, Dr. Umphrey Lee.

"Friend of all," . . . administrators, patrons, instructors, parents and students alike, his contributions to the great drama of life have been through deeds, not words.

It is then, in admiration and sincere appreciation that we gratefully and respectfully dedicate this book, *Rotunda* of 1945, to one whose stardom has given us genuine aspiration . . . to Dr. Umphrey Lee.

During the early years at SMU, the president bore almost the full burden of administration. He was in charge of public relations and finance, the internal administration of the university, and was the middleman between the trustees and the faculty. As Dr. Lee described it in 1948 in an address delivered at the inauguration of the Rev. Dr. Fred Garrison Holloway as President of Drew University, the university president is looked to for educational leadership but that leadership is complicated by the fact that he must "conduct a hotel, one or more restaurants, an investment service, a secretarial bureau, a mercantile establishment (usually a bookstore), a power plant, a park, a public relations office, an employment agency, and frequently an amusement concession." After all this has been attended to, his leisure time may be occupied by financial campaigns, public speeches, conferences with people who want to know why their children are not admitted or their friends not graduated. ("Our Educational Confusions.")

The year 1946 was probably one of the most difficult of Umphrey Lee's life as an administrator. With the end of World War II and the rapid return of our armies, the University changed quickly from a scarcity to an overabundance of students. The Veteran's Education Act enabled the backlog of college-age veterans to enroll at once. Older veterans who had missed college, and many who were cut adrift between army and civilian life, contributed to a new educational problem. The campus took on an entirely different complexion when 280 married veterans arrived on the campus and when, in April, Trailorville had its first birth—a boy.

It was a tense time, and the president was kept busy spiking rumors: There were too many students and the veterans with the lowest scholastic rating would be summarily dropped; the public housing authority would raise rents on the Trailorville units from $20 to $27 per month; the non-G.I.'s and coeds were complaining that the G.I.'s were so zealous about making good grades that the rest were having to work too hard to keep up with them. There were more males than females on the campus in 1947.

Dr. Lee always appeared calm and unhurried, but a glance at his engagement calendar would have dismayed most people who considered themselves restless and energetic. Not many of his activities got into the newspapers, but in 1946, the local papers reported a number of varied appearances. Included were graduation addresses at the end of each of the three trimesters, the Cole Lecture series at Vanderbilt University, speeches to the Dallas Club, the Methodist Men, the Richardson Rotarians, the SMU Alumni in San Antonio, and the Delta Sigma Phi banquet. He also conducted Palm Sunday vespers during Religious Emphasis Week and spoke at a rally for the Texas Country Day School Building Fund. He gave the principal address at the Memorial Service for the SMU war dead. He introduced Mayor Hocquard of Metz, France, at convocation, and he crowned the queen at the annual Homecoming football game. He presented the *Charm Magazine* award and gave his annual parties: the reception for the class of '21; for the faculty; and for freshman and transfer students. He was at the meeting of the Southern Association of Schools and Colleges in Memphis and helped celebrate Bishop Boaz's eightieth birthday at a dinner in Dallas.

VIII

" It's Real Hard Back in These Parts"

Months before Pearl Harbor, in the spring of 1941, there was pleasant excitement in the Lee family. Southern Methodist University's president was to have a new house. It was a welcome distraction from administrative duties to pore over plans and discuss the pros and cons of various arrangements and materials.

The remodeled president's house at 6001 Hillcrest Avenue was old, drafty—and the day Mrs. Lee discovered a snake coiled on one of the living room chairs, she decided that the time had come for a move. She and Dr. Lee began serious work on house plans. On September 10, property was purchased at 3600 Marquette and the dreamhouse begun. The *Dallas Morning News* reported that the house was to be completed by January 1, 1942, and was to cost $18,000.

The president's house, as it was finally built, followed the traditional southern pattern; two stories, tall white columns, wide entrance hall with stairway to upper rooms, living room and study to the right, dining room and kitchen to the left, and one bedroom with bath straight ahead.

Extra lighting was installed because of Dr. Lee's poor eyesight, and the walls of the study-library were covered with white-painted glass-front shelves; never enough room for all of Dr. Lee's books. Today the home of Mr. and Mrs. Umphrey Lee, Jr. in Louisburg, North Carolina, is almost a recreation of the study, living and dining rooms of the elder Lee's Marquette home. The two rose velvet barrel chairs frame the fireplace over which is the oil reproduction of a portrait of

John Wesley. There is the dark green Victorian occasional chair, the powder-blue wing chair, cream-colored sofa, wine Persian rug, a carved Victorian clock, crystal candelabra on the mantel, and elaborately carved Chinese table on which preside Chinese temple lions, and the leather-topped coffee table.

On the walls are paintings by Edward Beardon, Jerry Bywaters, and, in autumn gold and orange, a Colorado scene painted by Robert Shuttles, Jr. All were treasured gifts. Mary Lee was an avid antique hunter; Umphrey Lee, patient but usually less interested. However, Umphrey Lee's antique desk, now in his son's study, was one prize that he brought home from one of his wife's shopping trips in New Orleans. Over this desk hangs a favorite drawing of Dr. Lee done by Edward Beardon. Nearby is Dr. Lee's platform rocker, and the room spills over with books, including many fine old editions collected by Dr. Lee.

The dining room furniture was a favorite possession of Mary Lee's. It is now in Rose Lee's dining room, and the room is dominated by the silver service presented to the elder Lees by the Highland Park Methodist Church at the time they left for Vanderbilt.

The house at 3600 Marquette had a special wing on the far left built for Alberta Morgan, the Lees' longtime maid. Alberta Morgan was a part of the Lee family; she and grandmother Esther Lee took over much of Umphrey, Jr.'s upbringing. Esther Lee was shy, laconic, unexpressive. Like Calvin Coolidge, she specialized in one word answers. When her son asked one time what her preacher had talked about that morning, she answered, "Christianity." Trips to the church and cemetery were almost her only outside undertakings. Umphrey, Jr., when a little boy, sometimes went along with grandmother and an old lady friend on their trips to Josephus' grave in Restland Park in the friend's car.

The breach caused by Josephus and Esther Lee's opposition

to the marriage of Umphrey and Mary Lee was never completely healed. There was no quarrel, but mother and grandmother were always formal and rather distant. Mary Lee complained that Esther never said "Mary," but always referred to her as "she." But with little "Umphs," Esther Lee was kind and jolly and often sang to him folk ballads she had learned in the Kentucky hills, such as "Rain come wet me, sun come dry me, stand back pretty girl and don't come nigh me." Esther Lee lived with her son's family many years, but the last years of her life were spent happily in a nursing home where she seemed to find friends she enjoyed so much that she was reluctant to leave them even for a ride with her family. She died in 1947.

Possibly from Esther Lee came the humanizing simplicity that enabled Umphrey Lee, Sr. to remain "always the same" throughout his life. Friends who knew him from his early SMU school days until his death comment that he never changed. His character and personality remained the same no matter what his position or circumstance.

By the time the Lees moved back to Dallas and SMU, Umphrey, Jr. was eleven years old. He entered high school in September of 1940 and completed his work at McCallie School for boys in Chattanooga, Tennessee. Umphrey, Jr. always felt very close to his father and found in him an understanding parent when "Umphs" got into boyish scrapes. In his teens he seemed to be accident-prone. It was difficult to be the son of a prominent, admired father; and Umphrey, Jr. could not help feeling that he was always being compared unfavorably with his father. If Umphrey, Jr. ran away from home as a small boy or, later, backed his car into a neighbor's flower bed, bent an unsuspecting fender, or let some boy friend drive his car with disastrous results, everyone knew about it. But a call to his father always secured immediate cooperation. The wrong was righted, the annoyed were placated, and his

123

judgment of Umphrey, Jr. was a fair one. Umphrey, Jr., like his father, always felt a desire to teach and would gather the neighborhood children together to be his "class."

Holidays, special events, and traditional family-type customs, indulged in by some families, were ignored by the Lees, largely because Mary Lee objected to anything she considered too sentimental. "Umphs" was told that there was no Santa Claus from the very first. Only Christmas and birthdays were observed, and then father and mother showered Umphrey, Jr. with too many presents.

Alberta Morgan also had a hand in looking after the young Umphrey. She was devoted to Dr. and Mrs. Lee and had, in her wing of the house, a television set. For some unknown reason the Lees resisted getting television, but when some special program was on they would ask Alberta if they could come and watch it with her on her TV. Finally friends became concerned that the Lees had no TV set of their own, and Mrs. Tom Gooch gave them a monitor TV from the *Times Herald* TV station, KRLD.

There was not much time for wit and family jollity in the house at 3600 Marquette. The physical and mental pressures of the university presidency during the years of the war were great; Umphrey, Jr. was away in school, eventually he was in the armed services, and there was ample provocation for the more pessimistic Mary Lee to worry that some devastating catastrophe would overtake one of her precious Umphreys. She depended upon Umphrey, Sr. to reassure her that things were not so bad as they seemed.

Summer vacations spent in New Mexico and Colorado were relaxing interludes for the family. Dr. Lee taught Umphrey, Jr. how to fish in the mountain streams and how to ride. Once Dr. Lee's horse reared and fell backward on him, cracking several of his ribs. Many of Dr. Lee's speeches and writings utilize stories based on Rocky Mountain experiences. One such sermon had to do with fear and the virtue of coolness in the face of danger. Dr. Lee had felt justifiable pride in his son, and gratification in knowing that parental lectures were listened to, when Umphrey, Jr. came face to face with a bear, remembered his father's advice, and stood stolidly quiet until the bear turned and ambled away.

For several summers the Lees' favorite vacation spot was the W. B. Hamilton ranch in southern Colorado, but the summer of 1942, Mrs. Lee felt she should stay in Dallas where Umphrey Jr. was in summer school. Umphrey, Sr., greatly in need of rest and change after coping with the wartime problems, joined the Matchett family in Colorado.

The Matchetts had rented a cabin on the South St. Vrain River, an ideal location for dedicated fishermen. Umphrey Lee, Mr. Matchett, and the sons spent their days on the streams. After breakfast Dr. Lee and the men of the family fished in the vicinity of the cabin, returned for lunch and rest, and later in the afternoon were prepared for the serious fishing of the day when toward evening the fish are supposed to bite best.

Elizabeth Matchett Stover, one of the daughters of the family, recalls how much fun they all had during these Colorado summers and what a stimulating and agreeable companion Umphrey Lee was. His delightful humor sparkled every occasion, while reserve and dignity were also a part of him and enhanced rather than diminished his particular charm.

For ten months of each year the Lees' life was regulated by three little time-and-place records: an appointment calendar on Dr. Lee's desk; a duplicate on his secretary's desk; and the little black appointment book that was Dr. Lee's constant companion. It could breed catastrophe if the secretary made an error and the three did not coincide. Usually the remaining two months, July and August, provided relief from the strain of a feverish year. In Colorado Dr. Lee could "unwind." He seemed to draw strength from the mountains that enriched his life and fortified him for the coming hectic fall and winter.

Eventually the Lees bought a delightful two-story gleaming white Victorian house in the village of Georgetown, Colorado. The narrow house sported wood carving, gingerbread trim, and bay windows. An antique wrought-iron fence enclosed the property. Behind the house the mountains rose steeply.

Georgetown, about forty miles west of Denver, was more alive than many of the mining-era derelicts, striving for restoration without commercial contamination. It was a charming place nestled in the mountains and cherished the remains of some of its former glory, including the Hotel de Paris, preserved almost intact, and a house or two that were historical monuments. Georgetown had excellent antique shops that caught Mary Lee's practiced eye. It was she who had suggested that they buy the neat white house with its own rushing stream marking the back line of the property.

The Georgetown house was a great success. Dr. Lee found a fishing companion in the town's leading grocer. He counted himself fortunate to have a skilled fisherman friend and, also, a next-door neighbor who was an electrician and understood all the ills to which the charming old house was subject. That indispensable neighbor was described facetiously in one of Lee's newspaper columns as: "the paragon of all the virtues and the master of all the handy skills which enable your wife to use him as an example of what husbands should be." ("As I See It," September 8, 1956.)

In Georgetown, Dr. Lee thoroughly enjoyed himself fishing, reading detective stories, writing, chatting with neighbors, and occasionally donning an apron to help Mary Lee in the kitchen.

Visitors were regaled with humorous stories such as when Dr. Lee inadvertently got into a funeral procession on his way to officiate at a wedding. He was already late. When he finally extricated himself from the procession, half the mourners followed his car. It took something like a Keystone-cop chase to avoid arriving at the wedding trailed by the mourners. Another favorite story described his embarrassment when, as a very young minister in New York, he officiated at the wedding of a wealthy, socially prominent couple on Long Island. After the wedding and the reception, the parking attendants returned the cars to the door, and the butler in a basso profundo called out the name of each owner as his car arrived. Highly polished, elegant town cars arrived one after another to "Mr. and Mrs. Updike," "Lady Carlton," or someone equally impressive. Finally, up came an old Model-T Ford chugging and clunking along, and the butler boomed out, "The Reverend and Mrs. Lee." They hoped that they moved grandly down the steps into their old car.

The Georgetown area had many good restaurants, and the Lees knew them all. Dr. Lee was a large man and had a weight problem. It was difficult for him to diet. He appreciated good food and had to attend many dinners as the representative of SMU or as the featured speaker.

Once at his mountain retreat, Dr. Lee was hanging the week's washing on the line. He was dressed in his fishing clothes, "harmed by use"; he probably needed a shave. (Dr. Lee never shaved himself when a barber was near.) A lady, rather well dressed for the mountains, passed the Lee house and, with a tone of pity in her voice for the poor mountaineer, she exclaimed, "Life is hard, isn't it!" Dr. Lee, ever gracious, replied, "Yes Ma'am, it's real hard back in these parts."

Soon the Matchetts sold their house in Lyons, Colorado, and also bought a place in Georgetown. The delightful association of the two families continued as Mrs. Matchett, after the death of her husband, continued to spend her summers in Georgetown with one or more of her children.

During the summer of 1955, Umphrey, Jr. and his family visited the Lees in Colorado. After his service in the army as a paratrooper, Umphrey, Jr. had received his B.A. and M.A.

degrees from Stanford University and had entered Columbia University in New York City to begin work toward the Ph.D. On August 15, 1953, he was married to Rose Malone in the Louisburg Methodist Church in Louisburg, North Carolina. When Eleanor Malone Lee was born July 30, 1954, Dr. and Mrs. Lee became typically proud grandparents and were sent memberships in the Grandparents' Club. The next summer, Rose and Umphrey, Jr. brought ten-month-old "Nell" to Georgetown. With Dr. Lee driving, the young Lees were shown the wonders of Colorado. The next spring, on March 26, Umphrey Edwin Lee, known as "Buck," was born, and the young Lees did not go again to Colorado.

While savoring the pleasures of the relaxed mountain life, Dr. Lee also gathered material for his speeches and articles. One such favorite story, inspired by an experience in the pleasant old house, appeared in a later column in the *Dallas Times Herald,* a detective yarn with a moralism:

There have been some entries with burglarous and vandalistic intent in this little town in Colorado. . . . The other morning . . . I was awakened by a sound that resembled nothing so much as a working backward and forward of the key in my back door (not far from where I sleep). Since the lock could be opened by a teething child with a hair pin I was astonished that the work was not over sooner and that the sound persisted.

Finally, since I was never one to rush things, I managed to get up and stroll leisurely out to the kitchen. I was armed with nothing but a rifle which would stop a good-sized bear in his tracks; but I was brave and reasonably calm. My wife, who I supposed would stay in bed with her head covered up, as she was supposed to, suddenly bobbed up between me and the back door. I moved over to look out a window, and she got between me and the window. I remonstrated with a few quiet but well-chosen words and I thought she went back to her room. But when I tried to look out another room window later, secure in the confidence that my wife was safe in her room, I discovered that she was behind me and behind a door, where the slightest noise would have scared me into hysterics. . . . We at last decided the noises were probably from a mouse. . . .

Obviously I am not going to repeat this story where my friends will hear it. The picture of me parading around like a Revolutionary War sentinel trying to find a mouse and threatening his life and pursuit of happiness with a junior-size cannon, is not one that I care to perpetuate. But it did set me thinking. I wondered how many times in my life I had armed myself against major onslaughts which were in reality nothing more important than the playful scampering of mice.

Let it be said here and now that I am not easily scared. I always recall the old man who said that he could resist anything but temptation. I am never scared unless something threatens to attack me. But it is hard to know whether you are dodging mice or men. (August 25, 1957.)

Many Texas friends came to visit the Lees in Georgetown. Mr. and Mrs. J. Roscoe Golden, who had a summer home in another Colorado village, had been companions for many years. Mrs. Golden and Mrs. Lee enjoyed antique shopping expeditions together. Usually Dr. Lee was very patient with the leisurely pace of the antique hunters, but Mrs. Golden has a vivid recollection of one experience when she and Mrs. Lee lingered far too long over their browsing while Dr. Lee and Mr. Golden waited, first with patience and, finally, mounting irritation that caused Dr. Lee to lose his temper and express himself firmly to Mrs. Lee.

Dr. Lee's associates and family remember only rare instances of anger and then only when aroused with more than justifiable provocation. Umphrey, Jr. was impressed by his father's reluctance to criticize or condemn anyone. Dr. Lee would go to great lengths to find an explanation or excuse, even a very flimsy one, for another's unfortunate actions. But he had contempt for any form of humbug, hypocrisy, or cant and would, in the privacy of his family circle, sometimes express anger at someone guilty of the sin of great pride, which he termed egotism or "showing off." For a long time, until finally persuaded by the family, Dr. Lee would not hang the prized picture of John Wesley in his study, feeling that would be a form of bragging. He became quite angry one time about a gentleman who had turned down, with some publicity, a high office offered him. Dr. Lee felt that this man always had inordinate self-esteem, and that permitting an offer to be made to him, when he had no intention of taking it, was arrogance.

There were many pleasant aspects to life in Dallas. Dr. Lee took particular pleasure during the university year in his monthly meetings with the Town and Gown Club, a group of thirty SMU men and thirty from "town" who enjoyed good food, scholarly papers, and heated discussions. Town and Gown was organized in 1927, while Umphrey Lee was pastor at Highland Park Methodist Church, and the group felt that Dr. Lee's return to Dallas to become the president of Southern Methodist University gave them a more learned tone and greatly stimulated intellectual discourse.

Equally stimulating were sessions with "The Thirteen," a smaller group of the intelligentsia, also from both the University and the "town," who met regularly for erudite papers and learned discussions, a group held together by common interests and by a common catalytic, tantalizing wit. With "The Thirteen" every meeting was a fresh adventure. Perhaps Dr. Lee came as near to revealing his thoughts to this group as to any other.

Another more loosely organized group, calling themselves merrily The Lucullan Academy of Dallas, complete with fancy letterheads on their stationery, pretended to ignore the scholarly but concentrated on using their elusive sense of humor to add an additional sparkle to their Epicurean banquets far "from the madding crowd."

Dr. and Mrs. Lee were hospitable and charming hosts in Georgetown. In Dallas, both Mary Lee's aversion to formal entertaining and the press of professional or university-related activities precluded having many dinner or party guests in the president's home. The SMU University Woman's Club did, each year, have their fall tea welcoming new faculty wives in the president's house, and Mrs. Lee acted as hostess. Dr. and Mrs. Lee came to have a traditional Christmas party for Dr. Lee's immediate office personnel with their wives or husbands and, in the spring, a dinner in the home for the presidents of various student organizations and recognized campus leaders. These dinners were usually catered by the director of food services at the University, Mr. Gerald Ramsey.

There were other varied social activities. Some men felt that Dr. Lee was essentially "a man's man," and that he was at his charming best on fishing or hunting trips, steak fries, or evenings of good food and conversation when only men were present, frequently the same nucleus of close friends and occasional invited guests with a comparable share of intellectual curiosity and wit.

Without doubt, Dr. Lee was a great storyteller. There was never a boring moment in his society. A host of stories clustered around him, for he was master of that most elusive of qualities that makes a person entertaining company—conversational wit and humor matched with the right time and mode of utterance. J. B. Priestley is said to have eyes that have "the slight mesmeric quality of the born story teller." Umphrey Lee was, too, a born storyteller, but his eyes also had depth and kindness and a twinkle that invited "share the little joke with me." His wit was Shavian in its keenness but never caustic in tone.

One of his favorite stories was of the preacher who was called in at the very last minute to substitute at a funeral.

131

Somewhat breathlessly he seated himself facing the coffin. The choir at his back had begun to sing when it suddenly occurred to him that he had not been told whether the deceased was a man or woman. Since there had been no time to give him the name, he *did* need to have that much information. So he leaned surreptitiously toward one of the choir members and asked softly, "Brother or Sister?" The answer came back *sotto voce,* "Cousin."

Sometimes Dr. Lee went fishing at Bridgeport where Professor I. K. Stephens had a cabin. Almost every year for the last twelve of his life he hunted with his friend Paul Platter and a group, mostly non-university friends, that leased the hunting rights on a ranch in South Texas in an area called Loyal Valley, located between Mason and Fredericksburg. They were fond of a colorful hunting guide named Otto Keyser whose Uncle Herman had been captured by the Comanche Indians as a child. The hunting and tracking skills learned from his uncle were passed down from the Comanches.

Mrs. Lee was always solicitous of Dr. Lee's health. She went along on the first few of these hunting trips and became convinced that they gave Dr. Lee an opportunity to relax in the woods he loved and were good for him. When Dr. Lee joined the group, the men all stayed in a motel and did not rough it to the extent of camping in tents or sleeping bags, out of consideration for Dr. Lee's health. Tramping in the woods with devoted friends was Dr. Lee's greatest enjoyment on these expeditions. The least agreeable aspect with him was the early rising since he awoke slowly, a handicap on a hunting trip.

Hunting companions enjoyed and liked to quote examples of Lee's quick repartee. When he missed a shot, "Guess I used the wrong end of the gun"; when one of the men shot a deer that had a slight scar on its neck from an old bullet wound, "I saw that deer earlier as it passed me limping quite noticeably, but I didn't have the heart to shoot a deer walking with a cane";

when asked what he did when he had to attend so many dull sessions, "No trouble at all. I just throw my mind into neutral."

Through the Dallas years Dr. Lee's interests were varied, and the organizations to which he belonged reflected this diversification of interests. His schedule was exhausting, for he was frequently either a board member or an official in many of the organizations. He was president of the Civic Federation from 1930 to 1936; a member of the executive board of the Boy Scouts of America; on the board of trustees of the Dallas Health Museum; on the Citizen's Crime Commission; on the Dallas Council of Social Agencies; president and on the board of directors of the Rotary Club. Scholarly interests were reflected by membership in: The Medieval Academy of America; The Texas Historical Society; president of the Philosophical Society of Texas; and the Wesley Historical Society of England. He was a trustee of the Dallas Historical Society, on the board of the Dallas Symphony Society and, at one time, was president of the Southern University Conference.

The Lees together could be entertaining company. Mary Lee encouraged his humorous stories and, on occasion, added her own version of some amusing Umphreyabilia. Much good-natured bantering passed between them. Umphrey liked to tease Mary about her nonconformist brother who lived as he pleased; never worked consistently, just fished and hunted; and appeared unannounced at the Lees', off and on, in his disreputable old pick-up truck, wearing rough clothing. Dr. Lee was fascinated by the brother's irresponsible personality, admired his unrestrained use of the English language, and sometimes rescued him from a financial difficulty.

Not so funny at the time, but highly amusing later as one of his narrations, was Dr. Lee's experience borrowing his wife's car during the unusually heavy snow that fell on Texas in 1950 and remained on the ground for several days. Dr. Lee had driven to Austin but had been forced to leave his car and fly back to Dallas for a scheduled appearance. The next morning he borrowed Mary's car to drive to SMU, leaving it in the parking space reserved for the president behind Perkins Administration Building in the line of administrators' cars. But the sun came out, loosening an avalanche of ice and snow on the roof. Down with a crash came several hundred pounds of the frozen mass, all of it on Mary Lee's car, crushing in the top and doing great damage. "It doesn't pay to lend a car, even to your husband!"

This affectionate bantering sometimes was reflected in writing. In 1951, the following letter was received by Mr. Charles M. Powell:

> Dear Charles:
>
> When you helped us yesterday to get our car started, Mary and I were so busy in a private fight that I am not sure I even thanked you.
>
> My car stopped and I possibly flooded it. Mary began to give me detailed advice as to just how a car ought to be handled. At the same time she was trying to get out in the middle of traffic to get a garage to tow me in.
>
> I was quietly remonstrating with her at the top of my voice when you came up. You not only got my car started but you stopped troubles in which I was very definitely losing out.
>
> Sincerely yours,
>
> Umphrey Lee

No one could question Mary Lee's devotion to her husband and to his interests. He responded to her dependence on him with patience and affection. Dr. Lee once observed to his friend, Frank Story, "I just hope I can live longer than Mary. She really needs me." After his death, Mrs. Lee settled into a permanent melancholy that even her love for her children and grandchildren could not penetrate. With his death the light went out for Mary Lee, and her world was dark for the three years that she survived her husband. Soon after his death she left Dallas to join her son and his family in Louisburg, North Carolina, where Umphrey, Jr. is chairman of the department of English at Louisburg College. She died there in April 1961, and was buried beside Dr. Lee and his parents in Restland Memorial Park in Dallas.

Dr. Lee was gifted with that intuitive identification with the individual that enabled him to associate freely with people of widely divergent backgrounds and interests. His advice was widely sought. As president of SMU he received so many letters from distraught parents, urging him to have heart-to-heart talks with their sons and daughters or to intercede in parentally disapproved college romances that he could have devoted all his time to being an advisor to the lovelorn.

How did he draw people to him and keep their devotion? Partly because he was not a stereotyped, colorless, saintly character, nor was he guilty of what he called spiritual pride or irritating goodness. One felt that somewhere, somehow he must have an imperfection—he was so human, vitally warm and kind, qualities not always found in those in authority. Many people called him saintly; others have described him as a thoroughly civilized person, sensitive, reasonable, and essentially a gentle man. Thoroughly human, he could understand and empathize with the frailties of the less courageous.

IX

"Try to Think About Education"

In the late 1940's, Umphrey Lee came into the full stream of his activities as university president, teacher, writer, lecturer, religious leader, and civic figure. His established reputation as scholar and educator stimulated a deluge of invitations to speak in the United States and foreign countries. In 1945, the Australian Methodists invited him to Australia for a month to deliver a series of lectures under the Cato Lectureship Endowment. They were so eager to have him that they offered to make a four-months change in the date of the conference had he been able to absent himself from SMU in the immediate postwar period for that length of time.

In 1946, Dr. Lee was Cole lecturer at Vanderbilt University. In these lectures, published the next year in the small volume, *Render Unto the People,* we hear the mature Lee in polished prose discuss the present and future problems in the relations of "our kind of church—in this instance the Protestant Church —to our kind of state" (p. 5).

In 1947, there followed the Quillian Lectures at Emory University. In 1948, he gave the principal address when the Rev. Dr. Fred Garrison Holloway was inaugurated president of Drew University. In one of his most humorous lectures, SMU's president and educational satirist presented a university president's views on university presidents:

After a number of years in the presidential office of a university one is tempted to speak on the care and feeding of college presidents. On occasions when I have seen unsuspecting men led to the platform and entrusted with the seal of a university I have lamented the lack of a School for College Presidents, where they could learn some of the facts of life before entering upon their profession. But I suspect that a School for Those Who Endure College Presidents might be as helpful ("Our Educational Confusions").

With tongue in cheek, Dr. Lee continued in his inimitable satirical style, forsaking brevity to illustrate his point:

The college president will, of course, speak on all current issues, giving the public the advantages of his mature wisdom and the unusual insights which are expected of one in his position; and he will do this without offending the institution's constituency or provoking the faculty to reply to him. This requires, naturally, that the president will intuitively take the popular side of all questions. To do this he must retain certain qualities of the Boy Scouts which is difficult for his contemporaries: A president is "trustworthy, . . . helpful, friendly, courteous, . . . obedient, cheerful, thrifty, brave. . . ." The President must also be agile.

Then he commented on university benefactors: "The president might as well know from the beginning that, if no money is given to his institution, he is to blame. If money is given, someone else was responsible for the gift."

He elaborated on this point with an illustration of theories as to why the South lost the Civil War, as related to him by Dr. Horace Bishop, a former chairman of the board of trustees of SMU. It seemed that when anyone made a considerable gift to a university, several prominent men always claimed the responsibility. This reminded Dr. Bishop of all the arguments as to why the South lost the Civil War: shortages of men, money, etc. Dr. Horace Bishop observed that he, himself, "had always thought that the Yankees had something to do with it." Dr. Lee then pointed out that "in case of gifts to educational institutions, the donor should have *some* credit." Carrying the problems of money and meeting a pay roll further:

> Traditionally, the American college president is supposed to deal much in money. . . Faculty people are as concerned to receive their salaries as their better paid contemporaries. . . . But I have never believed that a president's only task is to go down town and come home with the bacon. . . . The president is supposed to maintain good relations between and among the trustees, the faculty, the students, persons who have given money to the university and persons who might give money to the institution.

Dr. Lee spoke at the Methodist Ecumenical Conference in Springfield, Massachusetts, in October 1947. He was guest preacher at the 138th session of the Mississippi Annual Conference of The Methodist Church in 1950; Alexander Gustavus Brown lecturer at Randolph-Macon College in 1953; Willson lecturer at Southwestern University and at Oklahoma City University in 1956; Willamette lecturer at Willamette University in 1956; Fondren lecturer at Southern Methodist University in 1957; and spoke as an educator to many other groups and organizations.

Along with a continuing effectiveness as a public speaker and writer, his good humor, charm, and wit became even more pronounced. Dr. Lee was obviously not only a scholar but an expert in the field of research. His writings are studded with apt quotations all properly annotated and ably illustrating the point he wished to make. In one particular lecture on the liberal arts college he refers to Paulus Vergerius and Vittorino da Feltre; and quotes Thomas Aquinas, A. E. Housman, Robert Hutchins, William Adams Brown, President Homer P. Rainey of the University of Texas, George Santayana, Theodore Meyer Greene, Ralph Barton Perry, George Willard Frazier, and Andrew Dickson White.

A remarkable memory and unusual ability to read and digest

material rapidly were responsible for his breadth of available knowledge. He could leaf quickly through a book, page by page, while standing, and then write a review of it. Keeping him supplied with books while he was hospitalized was an impossible task. This range of knowledge continually amazed people, as Paul Crume indicated in one of his columns:

Recently, two friends who were experts in the eighteenth century were talking with him at dinner. One of them mentioning the *Gentlemen's Magazine,* which still has a meaning for scholars, ventured that it was started in 1710. "Oh, much later than that," said the other. "1731," Dr. Lee, the amateur scholar, informed them, unconsciously.

A touch of humor, a clever turn of phrase, introduced most of these speeches on educational subjects. Speaking before the American Association of University Professors, SMU chapter, in 1940, Dr. Lee began:

Since almost every literate person in the United States has written at least one article on the Liberal Arts College, it would seem highly probable that this is one subject about which mature angels would walk lightly. There are enough of the rest of us, however, to keep the discussion alive. ("The Liberal Arts College Today.")

As the representative of colleges and universities at the Uniting Conference of The Methodist Church, he began:

I recall the exhortation of elders that a preacher should always be willing to speak as a dying man to a dying congregation. I am not clear that one should always be willing to speak to an expiring conference. But I am here under orders to represent the colleges and universities of united Methodism, some 140 of them, in fifteen minutes. . . .
Because of limitations in time I cannot clothe my statements in

adroit phrases and clever innuendoes. I shall have to say what I mean—a very unfortunate position for a college president.[1]

The purpose of education was discussed many times in Dr. Lee's writings, and "sometimes the college president will, with his faculty members, try to think about education." This exercise is, he says, likely to drive the college president mad, for each of the faculty advocates a different theory of education. Education is "intellectual discipline" to one, "personality development" to another. It is variously culture, citizenship, problem solving, wage-earning, maybe home planning. From this he concluded: "The modern educational controversy is one of the best examples of 'lo here' and 'lo there.'" ("Our Educational Confusions.")

He disposes of wage-earning as a sole aim of education by saying, "But the colleges do themselves no good by pretending that graduation is insurance of economic security. A sheepskin that had been blessed by a college president has no more magic potency than it had when it was attached to its original owner." ("Inaugural Address.") In the humanities, there is also the question of definition. One reputable authority, according to Lee, identifies the humanities curriculum as "these studies which inhumane teachers cannot completely dehumanize." ("The Liberal Arts College Today.")

A favorite illustration, when writing or speaking about education, was based on an experience in Colorado when he and one of his fishing and hunting companions, Paul Platter, set out to give Umphrey, Jr. the benefit of their fishing skill, developed over the years.

Two or three years ago I took part in an educational experiment in the State of Colorado. The conditions were presumably ideal:

[1] "Institutions of Higher Learning," *Journal of the Uniting Conference,* p. 901.

there were twice as many teachers as pupils, and the instruction was in connection with field work. A friend of mine and I undertook to teach a sixteen-year-old boy how to catch trout in a mountain lake.

The first lecture was concerned with the improbability of catching trout in a lake until a cloud had obscured the sun or until the wind had made ripples on the water. Before the first lecture was concluded, the pupil had cast a fly on the glassy surface of a sun-drenched lake and had caught a pound-and-a-half rainbow. Educators are accustomed to this kind of thing, and we were not daunted.

We entered immediately into the second lecture—that you must not cast for trout when they can see you. This lecture also was interrupted while the pupil landed another rainbow that had apparently been looking straight at the fisherman.

At this point lectures were suspended while the faculty retired to the other side of the lake and spent the rest of the day trying vainly to catch fish of their own. (*Render unto the People*, pp. 65-66.)

Lee, the humorist, then related his illustration to the point he wished to make:

I have mentioned this pedagogical experience to illustrate two facts concerning modern American education; first, that the educators are obviously confused about their own profession; and, second, that in spite of this some American boys and girls seem to be getting a fair education. One is especially grateful for the second fact when he is somewhat dazed with the multitude of books and articles on education.

He observed that many of the charges being hurled at our schools are unfounded but added that it is not easy for people to accept that the purpose of higher education is to develop and enrich the mind. There are all sorts of desirable side benefits; the providing of a place for matrimonial planning, the development of good sportsmanship, of teamwork, of bettering character, but, in his opinion, the main purpose is intellectual: "We need to learn to live as a group, to be well adjusted to the various duties and opportunities of life; but we also need to use our heads."

All the work of our predecessors, whether in science, literature, philosophy, art, religion or what not, is committed to us. Moreover, the teaching of the ways in which human beings use their most characteristic gift, that of intelligence, must be learned and taught. There is no substitute for ·it. There should be no apology for justifying the purpose of teaching. ("As I See It," March 2, 1958.)

Dr. Lee goes on to note that some educators have made the radical suggestion that girls who do not seriously want to use their education in a profession should be refused entrance to colleges as a means of reducing crowded conditions. These educators hold that space, time, and instruction should not be wasted on girls who have no use for college except as a dating bureau. He observes: "The remedy suggested is all right except that it does not go far enough: it ought to be applied equally to boys. . . . There is no use trying to cram an education down the throats of those who do not want it. The question of motivation is important; but for whatever reason, the vital question is: do they want it?" ("As I See It," March 2, 1958.)

Here he seems to indicate, not that he wants to discriminate against girls, but that it is not the function of the college or university to remotivate students who don't want college for the purpose of intellectual development, and that carrying them along is a handicap to more serious students.

Writing in 1957, Dr. Lee pointed out that we don't always vote with reason or buy with reason, and that formal education is not all the answer. "Some of the most intelligent people do not have much formal education. It might help if we paid more attention to teaching students how to assemble and assess the evidence and less time whipping up excitement on college campuses. . . . A child's remark put it well, 'If you don't use your head to think, it ain't no better than a baseball.' " ("As I See It," May 10, 1957.)

Relative to motivation, Dr. Lee repeated one humorous aprocryphal anecdote: A college dean told of the scholarship program in his college. Scholarship students who made A's received so much money; those whose average was B received a lesser monetary award. The dean then added: "Of course, this is a dreadful plan, totally unpedogogical. But, man, how it works!" ("As I See It," May 26, 1957.) That dean might be surprised to learn today that industry is using a variation of the plan to encourage employees to go to night school, repaying the entire tuition for A and part for each B grade.

As a historian and student of the classics, Lee had much to say about the role of the past in our educational scheme. He advocated that empirical data should be historically oriented but emphasized that this does not mean that we turn to the past only to learn how we happen to be what we are, but to learn the vastly important fact that there have been other ways of living than our own. "Most of the classicists," he said, "have known that men turned to Greek and Roman literature because for so many centuries there was no other source for the best works on politics, ethics, philosophy, economics, law and science. Men were always involved in contemporary problems but had to go to the only source they had for help." ("The Liberal Arts College Today," pp. 13-14.)

At various times during his years as a religious educator, Dr. Lee made observations regarding education in a changing society. He noted that older pedagogues felt that we were losing much in the passing of Latin and Greek. Dr. Lee's answer was that we would be losing much indeed if the study of Latin and Greek in the schools "opened doors to great literature where the students could browse to their heart's content." Unfortunately, he says, who has seen a college man or woman who "took Latin or Greek" and can "browse anywhere without help?" "We have not lost so much in the passing of Latin and Greek for the sad reason that we are not gaining so much by their stay." (*Jesus the Pioneer,* pp. 14-15.) Dr. Lee's own undergraduate education was in institutions which emphasized the classics, and he frequently deplored their passing for he was one who could "browse" in great literature. He was also one of the first education leaders to stress and use the term "academic excellence."

The lack of religious emphasis in education was also of concern to Umphrey Lee. In his youth at the turn of the century, as a round-faced, rosy-cheeked boy in Midwestern America, he probably mastered the spelling of "super-structure" at the same time he learned to recite the poem, "My Mother's Bible." But the educational scene changed, and the many editions of the "blue-backed" *American Spelling Book* and McGuffey's *Reader* were gradually replaced by texts which were more oriented to the educational philosophies of educators such as John Dewey. (Lee was spared Marshall McLuhan.) He regretted the passing of these old texts for one reason only —the old "Spellers" and "Readers" introduced religious and moral teaching without setting the religious apart from the secular, a point Dr. Lee pursued many a time in his career as a religious educator.

If the dichotomy between the religious and the secular was of some concern to him, so was the quality of some instruction in religious educational institutions: "It is my own conviction that a good deal of the teaching of religion on the college level in this country is directed toward . . . needs that were more common a generation ago than they are today." (*Render unto the People,* p. 110.) Two other points were expressed by Dr. Lee in regard to the interrelation of religion and education. One was the wish for "a more active representation of Christianity, and especially of Protestantism, in intellectual circles." The other was this candid observation: "It must be said in honesty that in this country Catholic scholars, when writing of Western culture, are much more likely to understand the place of religion than are those of Protestant backgrounds." (*Render unto the People,* p. 112 and pp. 108-9.)

The possibility of centralized control of education was viewed as a threat, and Dr. Lee felt that "federal control of education will come by way of the treasury." He made this point with penetrating humor: "I do not want to intrude into the field of Vergilian scholarship, but I suggest that the warning against the Greeks bearing gifts was called out not so much by the treacherous nature of the Greeks as by the inability of the Trojans to refuse anything that was free." (*Render unto the People,* pp. 100-101.)

The seeming decline of the private college or university was a profound worry. As early as 1939, Dr. Lee was analyzing the role of the private college and appealing for support. He addressed the Uniting Conference of the Methodist Churches in Kansas City as the representative of Methodist colleges and schools, saying:

The English theory was that the college stood in *loco parentis,* taking the place of the home in looking after the character and general welfare of the student as well as his mental development. The German theory of higher education was that the institution has no obligation to the student save intellectual. . . . To those who succumbed to this theory, the Church has no place in education.

He went on to reiterate that "the Church and the University are the two institutions of our time dedicated to the principles of human worth and human hope and they must not perish from the earth." Their durability was illustrated by the story of a man who was traveling in Georgia and saw some workmen building a church out of native stone. The passerby stopped, chatted with the men and asked them, "Do you think these stones will last?" One of the men looked at him quizzically and then replied, "Well, they've lasted 'til now." Dr. Lee's address ended, "And we have a sure Word which shall not pass away." ("Methodism's Institutions of Higher Learning.")

The Methodist Education Association, meeting in Philadelphia in 1940, heard Dr. Lee express his fear of state control of education and his belief that church colleges are a national asset. He proposed a plan for greater inter-institutional cooperation and coordination to eliminate duplication and ease financial strain. He spoke about the inadequate financial support given the church schools, pointing out that some had been saved from bankruptcy but then forgotten again. "It would seem that a Methodist college has financial appeal only when it is in full flight from the sheriff." ("Higher Education in United Methodism.")

At the Uniting Conference of the Methodist Churches, he had informed the delegates:

If the Church believes in her institutions, she should put enough money into them to enable them to do decent academic work—or she should close them. The fact that the president is a pious man and the faculty believe in prayer does not make up for poor laboratory and no books.

Skyscrapers do not stand up because the architect was a Methodist and bridges do not carry their load because the engineer's heart is pure. . . . There can be no substitution of piety for sound scholarship . . . and church colleges cannot inject religion as some sort of spiritual sulfanilamide. ("Institutions of Higher Learning.")

Again, two years later, in an article, "SMU—Present and Future," the importance of a dual system of colleges and universities is the basis for a plea for endowment and advancement.

Speaking before the National Chamber of Commerce in

1951, Lee made plain his position, stating that most businessmen do not realize that in higher education in this country
exists one of the greatest strongholds of freedom from government control. He maintained that a dual system of higher
education, part public and part private, is a healthy one since
they are subject to different pressures and inject the element
of free enterprise as a restraint on state control in education.
But sources of funds for private institutions seem to be drying
up and,

I do not need to attribute any sinister motives to anyone when I
say that one of the greatest influences for promoting the spirit of
freedom and of independence in this country will disappear when
half of all college and university graduates are no longer educated
at their own expense and at the expense of a liberal business
community, in an atmosphere untroubled by political pressures.
("These Bulwark Free Enterprise.")

In this same speech to businessmen, Lee warned:

If we bring up the next generation in a country in which health,
education, charitable relief, and old age are taken care of by the
government, you need not expect that business will be made a
grand exception. You cannot be saved by yourselves. If independent
education goes under, if the free professions go under, you haven't
a chance.

In 1947, Dr. Lee had written that he believed that the best
interests of both church and state would be served if the state
retained public funds for use in public education in elementary and secondary schools, "leaving aside perhaps questions of
textbooks, transportation and health services, letting the church
assume the extra cost for the extra services." (*Render unto
the People*, pp. 84-85.)

In 1950, he had reported to the board of trustees of SMU

that private education, in general, was in economic difficulty. He had recently attended a conference called by the American Council on Education and had discovered that other private colleges and universities were more and more striving to find a way to get federal funds.

By 1951, economic expediency had influenced Dr. Lee to modify his own views to recognize that, if private four-year colleges were to survive, some governmental help would be unavoidable. This he reluctantly admitted as he made this plain before the National Chamber of Commerce:

But in education also private enterprise is losing out. With higher costs, with the disappearance of great wealth *and* consequently of great patrons of education, and with competition from the apparently boundless pockets of state treasuries, the nongovernmental institution has come upon parlous times. And where can the independent educational institution turn?

On all sides the answer is being given: The State. It may be that the sources of income upon which private institutions have depended will dry up, that there will be nowhere to turn except to the government.

This address, given May 2, 1951, at the Statler Hotel in Washington, D.C., before the annual meeting of the Chamber of Commerce of the United States, was considered so important that it was read into the Congressional Record of May 15 by the Honorable Richard Bolling of Missouri in the House of Representatives and was also published in pamphlet form by the Chamber of Commerce.

At another time and before a Methodist assemblage, Dr. Lee admitted that church-controlled higher education could also have its dangers. He humorously conceded:

It must be admitted that there have been some unhappy occurrences when authorities have mistaken their ecclesiastical power for plenary inspiration concerning all things in the heavens above and in the earth beneath . . . and, in a few historic cases, in the water under the earth. ("Institutions of Higher Learning.")

Dr. Lee continued to decry the trend toward the elimination of any teaching of religion in public schools and colleges away from the past time when it was an incidental part of every course taught. The teaching of religion as an important part of our cultural development, both historically and as part of contemporary society, he considered essential to the main- tenance of a Christian society. He stated that Christian teachers have not kept abreast of Christian thought anymore than they have informed themselves about fields of learning other than their own and, so far as the courses in religion are concerned, Dr. Lee said, "it is doubtful whether the present-day student needs so much to be set right on the authorship of the book of Moses as upon the importance of religion and its place in life." (*Render unto the People,* p. 110.)

By 1958, Lee was recommending that the church follow its own students to state-controlled universities, and that more care should be taken to see that the Wesley foundations pro- vided "serious teaching by competent people on the state campuses." (*For the Rising Generation.*)

The fact that "we can no longer believe that educational 'laissez faire' will provide a beautiful world in which the lamb, with an atom bomb in its possession, will lie down peacefully with the lion" (*Render unto the People,* p. 96) made it obvious to Dr. Lee that overhauling and more planning were needed in the universities. A recognized defect was that the students were introduced to so many disparate fields of learning. The student could not see any connection for the obvious reason that there is no connection. American academicians have long thought only in terms of departments and courses, but a man is not educated just because he has had English I or Chemistry

I or built up sufficient numbers of courses to have a major; but the educated man is one who has a unification of knowledge for, "We can adjust ourselves to the times only when we have a large enough horizon that we can see things in their proper proportions." (Lee, *Jesus the Pioneer,* p. 38.)

As early as 1940, Dr. Lee was recommending changes in the university curriculum of the Liberal Arts College that are only recently beginning to be implemented, specifically:

(1) A course in general science for the non-majors who need to know the nature of the sciences, the scientific method and the relation of these to modern life;

(2) The acceptance of the college's responsibility to teach the student to speak and write English, if the secondary school has not done so;

(3) The development of language, apart from literature, as a tool. Having passed foreign language courses should not be the criterion;

(4) The requirement of two years or twelve semester hours in "a comparative study of the literature, history and arts of other cultures." This should be a genuine study of culture epochs so that the student can understand the development of modern western culture, the interrelations of social situations, philosophy, ethics, theories of government, expressions in art and literature, economic theory, religion, and the accompanying theories of man and the world, so that one would learn the constant interaction and interrelation of the different elements in a culture;

(5) Less majoring in a single department but substitution of some majors that would cut across divisions. An example was Victorian literature with knowledge of the history, economics, and government of the period. ("The Liberal Arts College Today.")

As a non-ivory-tower scholar and student of the current scene, Dr. Lee anticipated so well the trend of the times that a miscalculation is doubly interesting. Writing in the *Dallas Times Herald* in 1958, he devoted his column on two Sundays to the need for more scientists and mathematicians. He was pessimistic about attracting the young into these fields because they were time consumers that ruined play and popularity, are branded as egg-head occupations without status, and do not offer enough in monetary reward! ("As I See It," January 5 and 12, 1958.)

X

"Well, Why Didn't You Say So?"

As years went by and more and more sermons were preached, more and more speeches were made, and more and more articles were written, the pithy statement, the clever turn of phrase, the witty example appear more and more frequently. With maturity and status Dr. Lee, at last, gave almost free rein to those delightful qualities that were held in check in earlier, more uncertain youthful days.

The appearance on the platform of this dignified man with his smiling face and slightly rumpled figure immediately alerted an audience; they learned to watch, with delicious anticipation, for the sparkle in the eye presaging some remark of gentle wit and worldly wisdom characteristic of the Lee style. The published speeches or his own manuscripts do not do full justice to this style. The twinkle in the eye, the intonation of voice, the unpublished phrase, and the intuitive timing all contributed to a heightened effectiveness that defied transcription.

Umphrey Lee was as skilled at pulpit oratory as at classroom lecturing or civic address. He moved with ease and a high degree of rhetorical skill from one of these diverse speaking situations to the other, always achieving a high degree of consistency in favorable audience reaction. He was as much in demand as a speaker from educational institutions as he was religious and civic organizations for a period of over thirty years, from 1924 until his death in 1958. He wrote all his speeches and never utilized a ghost writer. He was inventive and original. The viewpoints and syntax were his own. When he wrote the speech in longhand, it became necessary for his

152

secretaries to develop their own Rosetta stone system to decipher the Lee hieroglyphics.

Dr. Hemphill Hosford recalls seeing Dr. Lee many times huddled over a typewriter rapidly "hunting and pecking" out the first draft of a speech.

On several occasions, Dr. Hosford followed Lee's address with one of these manuscripts and found that Lee, without a manuscript but with a few hastily scribbled outline notes on the back of an envelope, delivered the address almost verbatim, speaking in his distinctive conversational, informal style. He must have possessed almost total recall or, possibly, a photographic memory, since his study of the manuscript before giving his speeches was usually brief.

However, Lee's ability to recall many pages of script did not affect the style of his delivery, which never gave the impression of being stilted or memorized. Formal oratory was not for him; consequently, his audiences felt they were hearing a highly skilled extemporaneous speaker. Invariably the effect was one of spontaneity and informality. He spoke with all the assurance and ease of a man speaking to one person in that person's own living room. He rarely used gestures. The "I'm interested in you" attitude facilitated this immediate rapport with an audience. His skill was even more remarkable since his sermons or speeches were so carefully researched, outlined, and polished.

As a matter of fact, he was an excellent extemporaneous speaker, but seldom did he rely on this ability. He once confided to Hosford, "I never made a speech without thoroughly preparing for it, except on one occasion, and that was a failure."

In the later years of his presidency at SMU, Dr. Lee used a dictograph machine since the demand for him as a speaker was enormous. When out of town, he sent the records to his secretary to be typed. Time no longer permitted his "hunt and peck" method. Advance copies were sent to the news media, not only as a courtesy, but for another reason. While he liked and maintained cordial relations with gentlemen of the press, their ability at correct recall was to him suspect. He also looked with a jaundiced eye on their stenographic abilities.

Dr. Lee suffered, as do most successful speakers, from stage fright, apparently a necessary evil for effective public address. Dr. Richard Smith, family physician and close personal friend of the Lee family, once observed to Dr. Lee, "You know, Umphrey, I never get up to make a speech without a feeling of nervousness," and Lee replied, "Neither do I." He once confided to his choir director at Highland Park Methodist Church, Mrs. J. Roscoe Golden, that he suffered inevitably from bouts with that speaker's plague. To Mrs. Golden who had noted that he always seemed to be nervous before delivering his sermons, as she was before singing, he said, "I'll tell you one thing, if we ever get over it, we both better stop."

In one of his Sunday columns, with some authority after many years on the speaker's platform, he wrote of those "first awful minutes when you face an audience—no matter how long you have been making speeches." ("As I See It," March 3, 1957.)

A fine voice, flexible, resonant, commanding, was utilized by Umphrey Lee to its fullest potential. There was a variety of pitch, tempo, force, and volume in his delivery, and yet the overall effect was one of the most natural of delivery styles. He never resorted to the florid pulpit tone or cadence. He maintained that he followed the advice of a "good old lady" who once reproved him for speaking over the audience's head and using obscure terminology. She taught him a lesson regarding simplicity and clarity of word choice which he never forgot. It seems that the "good old lady" came up to him after church and asked what he meant by a particular word. He told her. She responded indignantly, "Well, why didn't you say so?" ("As I See It," December 8, 1957.)

Vocabulary was always adapted to the audience. Lee had at his command the jargon of a surprising number of professions and businesses, and he could speak to theologians, educators, doctors, cotton growers, salesmen, or Rotarians in their own terminology, often to the amazement of his audience.

At times he showed a sense of the poetical as in the Easter message in which he paraphrased the Venerable Bede on an Anglo-Saxon pagan's idea of immortality: 'Man is like a bird flying out of the darkness and cold of winter into a lighted and heated room. He is there but a moment and he flies out again into the cold and darkness. . . . He came out of darkness and into darkness he returned." ("As I See It," April 21, 1957.) Relating this illustration to the point of his message, Dr. Lee concluded, "The builders of cathedrals and their successors today . . . are not satisfied with mere immortality, a simple going on and on. They want to take the light and warmth with them. . . . They thought of a time when their youth and strength might live again."

In a lecture in 1943, he advanced a definition which might be utilized as a pragmatic theory for successful communication:

Definitions are admittedly not fashionable. . . . But some people, reasonably or not, when they are invited to a discussion prefer to know what is being discussed. And those who think this academic fussiness forget that, if one cannot settle the question by defining some disputed term, he can at least say what he means and try to mean the same thing for fifteen minutes. ("The Spiritual Basis of Democracy.")

He defined speech as "a means of communicating ideas— not a means of concealing them." ("As I See It," December 8, 1957.) In the tradition of S. I. Hayakawa and other general semanticists, he offered this illustration of the problems in communication:

Recently I remarked to a friend that a certain man would not work in the "off"; but my friend did not know anything about driving horses, and I had to explain my metaphor. . . . I forgot that only those who share the same experiences can share the same language. ("The Community of the Confident.")

In regard to semantic difficulties, he once remarked about "the inexactitude of our language usage." He felt that most of man's problems with symbols and their meaning are, in part, due to the "haste with which much is said and written," in addition to the fact that very often "the speaker or writer did not know what he meant to say in the first place."

A particularly fine sense of language was exemplified in the delicate use of humor to emphasize a point and fix it in the listener's memory. It might be a word, a phrase, or an anecdote. It could never be said of Umphrey Lee, as of one famous wit of the past, that "he would rather make an epigram than a friend," for his wit was gentle and placed an audience in his command. He possessed an almost uncanny knack for selecting and adapting the appropriate humorous story to the audience.

At a Methodist conference, the question arose as to the advisability of deleting from the Order for the Consecration of Bishop, "Are you persuaded that you are truly called to this ministration, according to the will of our Lord Jesus Christ?" Lee rejoined, "Let's leave it in, someone might say no!" After the laughter had subsided, the committee agreed to take his advice and not delete the phrase.

To an audience of theological students, he observed, regarding theology by majority vote of religious bodies: "A long time ago someone remarked, concerning this idea of understanding the will of God by majority vote, that the Holy Ghost had to be the odd man." (*Render unto the People*, p. 123.)

In his inaugural address to an audience of students and educators, he maintained that the college curriculum was indeed related to everyday life, since, "As someone said recently, the man who is run over by an automobile today has really been run over by mathematics, physics, and chemistry, or— to put it another way—by Euclid, Archimedes, and Lavoisier."

As SMU's chancellor, in a Fondren Lecture, he expressed amusement at our efforts to break with the past as revealed in the popularity of the Scandinavian-like roofs of modern church architecture in Texas: "The Scandinavians built their steep roofs to keep the snow off. And we build them down here in Texas where there's not enough snow to embarrass a rose bush."

Another religious leader, possessing less diplomacy than Dr. Lee, marched next to Lee as the administration and faculty filed into the auditorium in academic robes for a formal convocation. The other gentleman's degree was from Yale; Dr. Lee's was from Columbia. Lee's partner in the academic "lineup" heartily exclaimed, "Umphrey, congratulations on your recent honor—such as it is." Lee repeated the story many times, especially when addressing educators. He never thought of himself as important.

The Rev. Mr. Lee, humorist and social commentator, in the sermon, "Light of the World," declared:

A writer in a recent magazine says that business men are beginning to show a new humility. Personally, I have not noticed this prevailing to any great extent, but I am glad to receive evidence. . . . We know that educational theorists are losing a little of their old self-confidence—not much, perhaps, but a little of that swaggering smugness which characterized many before-the-war educational men. I say nothing of preachers. I fear that it will take more than a world war to bring humility to some of us. (*Jesus the Pioneer,* p. 72.)

Humor often appeared in the introduction to a sermon. He revealed something of the iconoclast when he described, in a Mother's Day sermon, a "little gray-haired mother" who lived in a "vine-clad" cottage as being as scarce "as a dodo." Our sentimental tears on Mother's Day reminded him of Maria Theresia of Austria who, when the powers gleefully were carving up Poland, "was much distressed at the fate of the unhappy kingdom; but Frederick the Great remarked that 'she wept, but she kept taking.' " (*Jesus the Pioneer*, pp. 42-43.)

Dr. Lee's repertory of old preacher anecdotes reflects not only his experience as a pastor, but his early life as a preacher's son and a preacher's grandson:

I knew a few wise old preachers who never talked about anything but the orphans [when taking collections for church expenses]. Only a small part of the "conference collections" went to the orphans, but the old preachers I am talking about never discussed education or missions or certainly not administrative expenses.

They talked about the poor orphans, and if a man objected to education or missions or bishops' salaries, he was by implication a man who would not open his pocketbook to help the orphans. It was perhaps not exactly an honest method, but it worked. ("As I See It," February 2, 1958.)

In one lecture, Lee observed that psychologists were placing a great deal of emphasis upon the influence of childhood experiences on adult behavior:

Recently I confessed to a friend, a psychologist, that I seemed instinctively to dislike a certain man. My friend suggested that this dislike might arise from some forgotten childhood experience; I might even, he thought, have been bitten by a dog which in some way resembled this man. I admitted the likeness, but as a confirmed dog lover, I rejected the suggestion. (*Render unto the People,* p. 89.)

Dr. Lee's range of interest was as wide as his humorous summations were brief. On Englishmen: "Some believe that an Englishman changes his mind with the speed of a glacier"

(*Render unto the People,* p. 46) ; on football: "About the only unified integrated program on the campus" (*Ibid.,* p. 108) ; on tact: "Sometimes a compliment is of more help than a tranquilizer" (unpublished).

A precise choice of words enabled him to depict vividly the point which he wished to make, with the utmost clarity. He expounded on the idea of first things first by stating, "When the winds blow and the floods descend, the question is whether the house will stand, not whether the interior decorator has fumbled his colors." ("The Spiritual Basis of Democracy.")

He also had something to say regarding self-improvement: "Few people make fools out of themselves. Most of them simply make improvements or alterations." ("As I See It," April 14, 1957.) On the pitfalls of political power he commented: "The devil may have exaggerated a bit when he claimed to control all the kingdoms of the world, but he did know what is likely to happen to those who gain political power." (*Render unto the People,* p. 138.)

Lee once referred to beards as "pioneer shrubbery," and furthermore, "In the end, a mouse behind a beard is probably still a mouse." ("As I See It," June 2, 1957.) He observed that an accurate analysis of one's capabilities was a most desirable trait to possess and that some voices were meant for the chorus, others for the concert stage, and, "In the same way most people will never be rich. I do not believe that it will hurt them to acknowledge this fact to themselves. It would be a good idea if their wives knew it." ("As I See It," September 16, 1956.)

He advised doctors on diplomacy in the following manner: "In this country the best way for a doctor to make a living is not to greet his patients with the announcement that they probably have hydrophobia—although it may turn out to be a common cold. People come to expect a ray of light, if possible even a little hope, from their doctors. If he can't stand to hear about their pains, how does he expect his patients to bear them?" ("As I See It," April 14, 1957.)

The list of "quotables" is almost inexhaustible. A few more follow. He told of a friend who had been reading Cicero's essay on old age; the friend informed his cook: " 'Cicero says that old age is the finest time of life.' Nannie went on with her work, but made her contribution to Ciceronian scholarship: 'I don't know Mr. Cicero, but I'll bet he has money.' " He concluded that "The Ciceros of this world are a good deal more cheerful than they would be if they didn't have money." ("As I See It," December 9, 1956.)

In his later years he often mused about old age: "I like the American habit of exaggerating one's virtues, even when, as I grow older, I don't believe what I hear." ("As I See It," February 16, 1958.)

"What they are at 80 is what they were at 40 . . . and you don't develop character by learning a hobby at 65." ("As I See It," October 28, 1956.)

"John Wesley lived a long time . . . long enough to change his mind." (*Our Fathers and Us,* p. 62.)

"A friend of mine overheard a freshman girl at a sorority party say to a friend: 'I want you to meet my uncle. He is 35, but he is still active.' " ("As I See It," October 28, 1956.)

On the same subject of old age, he presented his version of the superannuated cliché: "Two of the greatest moral influences are old age and rheumatism." ("As I See It," October 28, 1956.)

Dr. Lee's fellow historian and devoted friend, Dr. Herbert Gambrell, described his former boss as having a "tongue that used language to express, not to obscure thought," and he added, "No man of his generation was more eagerly sought as speaker, dinner guest, or companion." [1] He was a "good man speaking well."

[1] Gambrell in Lee, *Our Fathers and Us,* p. vii.

XI

The Short-handled Shovels
Tied with Red and Blue Ribbons

A famous jurist once wrote:

Money alone, however, could not build a university: . . . To be
great, a university must express the people whom it serves, and must
express the people and the community at their best. The aim must
be high and the vision broad; the goal seemingly attainable but
beyond immediate reach. . . . The university's life and soul is the
faculty. Laboratories, books, and endowment—only the essential
tools.[1]

Dr. Lee's emphasis on academic excellence and his unre-
lenting efforts to add more professors of distinction somewhat
obscured the extent of his activity in securing the funds and
the tools to implement his plan to make Southern Methodist
a great university.

Although Umphrey Lee had been pastor of two congregations
that had built churches during his tenure, he was not primarily
a money raiser. The aggressive approach in anything was
anathema to him. This was so well understood that his ministerial friends in the conference made a running joke of insisting that he should be put on the Commission on Evangelism
(now the Board of Evangelism) of the church, implying that
this was the last place he should be. His approach was definitely "low-pressure," and probably many gifts to SMU were

[1] Alpheus Thomas Mason, *Brandeis*, p. 589.

unsolicited and reflected the confidence of the donors in Dr. Lee.

The late 1940's and 1950's "rained" buildings at SMU. During Dr. Lee's tenure as president the Fondren Library was completed and nineteen other permanent buildings were begun. Only two of them, the Joseph Wylie Fincher Memorial Building and the Umphrey Lee Student Center, were dedicated after his resignation from the presidency in 1954.

The short-handled shovels tied with red and blue ribbon, SMU's colors, came out regularly for ground breaking, followed in due time by appropriate ceremonies for cornerstone layings and then dedications with public honors and sincere private expressions of appreciation for generous donors. In May 1951, Dr. Lee reported to the board of trustees, "In the last twelve months we have opened and dedicated eleven buildings at a cost of $7,500,000."

The real avalanche of buildings, after Dr. Lee assumed the presidency, was touched off by a large gift from Mr. and Mrs. Joe J. Perkins. As told by Bishop Paul E. Martin at a luncheon of Perkins School of Theology Alumni at SMU, February 3, 1965:

Tuesday afternoon, June 13, 1944, following the afternoon session of the Jurisdictional Conference [in Tulsa], a group met in the hotel room of Mr. and Mrs. Perkins. . . . In addition . . . were Dr. Umphrey Lee, Bishop A. Frank Smith, Mildred [Mrs. Martin] and I [Bishop Paul E. Martin]. . . . This was the time in which the project definitely came into being although the announcement was not made until several months later. . . . This meeting that afternoon in the Mayo Hotel in Tulsa was of great significance.[2]

The original gift, announced in February 1945, for the Southern Methodist University School of Theology, was $1,350,000. It was increased by $2,000,000 in 1946. Total Per-

---

[2] Walter N. Vernon, *Methodism Moves Across North Texas*, p. 242.

kins gifts to SMU eventually reached $10,000,000, and the Perkins name is perpetuated on the campus in Perkins Hall of Administration, Joe Perkins Natatorium, Perkins Chapel, Lois Perkins Auditorium in Selecman Hall (a Perkins gift), and S. B. Perkins Hall. The University's original theology building had been the gift of Harper and Annie Kirby of Austin. This became Florence Hall in the Law quadrangle when the University constructed a new building in the Theology quadrangle to carry the Kirby name. Later J. S. Bridwell and daughter Margaret of Wichita Falls gave Bridwell Library in the Theology quadrangle.

In 1946, Mrs. W. W. Fondren wrote to the board of trustees that she "was working out a program whereby a gift of $1,000,000 in cash and property will be made available to SMU for use in the erection of a new science building." This was one of many Fondren gifts that included Fondren Library, Fondren Lectures, and Fondren scholarships.

Following is a list of the major buildings completed or begun during Dr. Lee's presidency:

1. Fondren Library—completed 1940
2. Joe Perkins Natatorium—1942
3. Lettermen's Memorial Dorm—1947
4. Engineering Laboratory #1—1947
5. Caruth Engineering Building—1948
6. Fondren Science Building—1950
7. Peyton Hall Dormitory—1950
8. Robert Storey Hall (Law quadrangle)—1951
9. Lawyer's Inn—1951
10. Engineering Laboratory #2—1951
11. A. Frank Smith Hall (Theology quadrangle)—1951
12. S. B. Perkins Hall (Theology quadrangle)—1951
13. Paul E. Martin Apts. (Theology quadrangle)—1951
14. Eugene B. Hawk Apts. (Theology quadrangle)—1951

15. Perkins Chapel (Theology quadrangle) —1951
16. Bridwell Library (Theology quadrangle) —1951
17. Harper and Annie Kirby Hall (Theology quadrangle)
    —1951
18. Selecman Hall (Theology quadrangle) —1954
19. Joseph Wylie Fincher Memorial Building—dedicated
    November 4, 1954
20. Umphrey Lee Student Center—begun 1953

In 1947, Hare and Hare, Kansas City architects and city
planners, were commissioned to prepare a master plan for the
campus, and a definite attempt at beautification, suspended
during the war, was begun. The old Southern Methodist University Southern Pacific spur, called Soumethun, laid in 1912,
to connect the Dallas Hall site and the steam plant with coal
and lumber yards, was finally torn up in 1941. The material
for the Fondren Library was the last to be carried over the line.

As president of the student's association in 1915-16, Umphrey
Lee had been one of the promoters of the first campus beautification campaign; he recognized that aesthetic standards were
not "mere luxuries" but important adjuncts in an educational
institution. The campus was no model of beauty during and
after the war. First there was a shortage of money and personnel
to care for the grounds, and, later, there were ugly temporary
buildings and the scars of construction.

At one of the meetings of the board of trustees Dr. Lee
commented on the seemingly interminable disruptions. His
little story involved his conversation with a downtown luncheon companion. After complaining about the torn-up streets
in Dallas and on the campus, he quoted himself as saying,
"It would be good to live sometime in a town that has been
finished." The luncheon companion, who was a visiting Scot,
answered, "In Scotland, the town I came from was finished

300 years ago. I don't think you would like it." So Dr. Lee decided that maybe it is "not so bad to work where work is never complete."

Although several million dollars from many donors flowed into the coffers of SMU for buildings and other campus improvements, the problems of endowment and ready cash for operating expenses remained acute. The yearly Sustentation Fund Drive, returns from SMU's relatively small endowment, and tuition payments were insufficient to support the fine plant developing on the campus. Too often the yearly budget showed a deficit, and the president could never be relieved of the worry about money. Budgeting was hazardous because of the uncertain enrollment. The World War II decline in student population was followed by the postwar oversupply; another decline set in as veterans left school; then came the effects of the low birthrate of depression years; and, finally, the Korean War effected a drop in enrollment. At the same time, the growing reputation of the University began to attract more freshmen from the high schools, but not enough to balance the loss as upper classmen had to leave.

Funds were always in short supply, but in 1945, the board of trustees sadly declined to accept a check for several thousands of dollars presented by 100 of the retail liquor dealers of Dallas. Umphrey Lee, Jr. humorously relates that an SMU professor's daughter, with whom he was in love at the time, thought that SMU should take the money and tried to put pressure on Dr. Lee through the son. She was so persuasive that Umphrey, Jr. did try unsuccessfully "to work on" his father who explained that, although he did not subscribe to the theory of "tainted money," acceptance would do more harm than good.

Further excitement was generated in 1949, over a newspaper story that George Armstrong, a Fort Worth millionaire, had offered $5,000,000 if Jews were barred from admittance. Dr. Lee issued a denial that any such definite offer had been made,

165

adding, "It is perhaps unnecessary to say that if such an offer had been made it would have been declined."

Faculty conflicts were as numerous as student conflicts, and in the 1940's when Southern Methodist University was still operating under the "one-big-family" plan of organization that had sufficed in the prewar small school, all problems passed over the president's desk. In a speech at Drew University, Dr. Lee commented on the closely knit life of faculties on a college campus: "A Catholic priest once told me that there is a saying that those who have lived at a common table are passed straight into heaven when they die because they have already had their purgatory." He mused on professors: "One or two of them may keep a president busy defending them because of speeches they never would have made if they had been making their living any way other than by teaching." ("Our Educational Confusions.")

When Dr. Lee became president of SMU he began his policy of spelling out to the board of trustees his concept of the needs and aims of the University. His first report emphasized that SMU should not try for "mass education" but aim for a medium enrollment of a stated number and high educational quality. Later he suggested a gradual increase in admission requirements; addition of distinguished faculty; and a major curriculum revision for the College of Arts and Science to assure "a broader and deeper education to those who leave this college."

In his first report he enumerated: physical plant needs, including buildings for science, business, and law; funds for yearly operating expenses; and endowment. In the spring of 1944, he suggested to the board of trustees that the time was ripe for a campaign for endowment, emphasizing his belief in the function of the private or church-supported colleges in balancing the state schools. He believed it was a crucial hour for

SMU and its future in the Southwest. His report had this closing appeal:

If we can go forward now, we shall do for this institution, for which so many of us have long labored, that which John Wesley put into words when he sent George Shadford to America. "George," he said, "I let you loose on the great continent of America. Publish your message in the open face of the sun and do all the good you can."

He began to talk of the need for a permanent student union building and spoke of the hopes of creating a fine library at SMU. He believed that the library was the heart of the university. Dr. Lee had always spent much time in the library. Mrs. Grace Teague, librarian at the Vanderbilt School of Religion when Dr. Lee was the dean, compared Dr. Lee with other deans, saying that the usual practice was for the dean to send his secretary to the library for any books he needed, but "when Dr. Lee wanted a book, he came himself, and one had to be careful not to trip over him as he squatted between the stacks, reading." By 1951 Bridwell Library in the SMU School of Theology was described as housing one of the best theological collections in the country.

In 1947, SMU entrance requirements were tightened so that high school graduates in the lower fifty percent of their class would have to take entrance examinations.

Dr. Lee's thinking kept returning to the point from which it started: how to develop an intellectual climate at Southern Methodist University that would, in time, raise it to the level of a great university. He began to urge that SMU could not wait longer to increase its faculty of "distinguished scholars of national reputation as the course to building a great university." He urged haste: "I do not know whether it is true that opportunity knocks but once, but my experience is that in the Southwest one had better not wait even for the first

167

knock; it is safer to get the door open while opportunity is wiping his feet on the mat and looking for the bell." (Report to the Board of Trustees, 1947.)

By 1949, he could report that the freshman class was holding up in enrollment and that more and more of them were from the upper quartile of their high school class. At the November 11 meeting of the board of trustees he attempted to articulate his idea of the duty of the Board and the administration:

It is our task, therefore, as I see it, to provide the physical plant, to provide the funds with which this university can operate, and to find the men whom we think wise enough to carry out our thinking program. Of course, we are going to shape the course of things along the lines that seem best to us. It is inevitable and right that we invite to these faculties men whose opinions seem to us to be sound.

In doing this we shall color the university and to a certain extent determine its nature; but when we have done all this, let us turn the university over to our successors with full confidence that they will be able to take care of their generation as well as we have taken care of ours, and let us turn over to them an institution which is as little encumbered with dead hands as we can possibly make it.

Dr. Lee was not the hard-driving, overorganized administrator who is the stereotype of the leaders of large enterprises today. His contact was personal and individual. The inter-office memo was unknown, and he rarely, if ever, called meetings of his deans or reduced to writing the decisions and plans he discussed with his associates. Members of his board of trustees remember that their relationship wth him was one of perfect confidence and friendship. There was never any conflict. President Lee kept in close contact with the chairman of the board of trustees, Bishop A. Frank Smith, whom he had known since college days; and the chairman of the executive committee of the board of trustees, Mr. Eugene McElvaney, who had been a freshman at SMU when Umphrey Lee was a graduate student and who had become his parishioner and friend when the Rev. Umphrey Lee returned to Dallas as pastor of the Highland Park Methodist Church.

The telephone was a valuable tool for Dr. Lee, and calls to Bishop Smith in Houston and Mr. McElvaney at the First National Bank in Dallas were frequent. Vital matters had been discussed and a presentation was well in hand before the semiannual meeting of the full board of trustees and the much more frequent meetings of the executive committee.

In 1947, Dr. Lee was made chairman of the Listening Post Committee of the George Foster Peabody Awards for Dallas (one of 92 cities) to recommend programs and stations for awards to the National Broadcasting Company. Dr. Lee was to select his committee. There is no record of the accomplishments of this committee. Presumably he secured members with an interest in radio and time to indulge it. A glance at a list of Dr. Lee's activities makes it clear that he had little time for dial twirling. When asked how he found time to do all the things he accomplished, Dr. Lee replied, "Well, I think of all the fool things I do. And I just whittle off some of the fool things. And I have time for whatever needs to be done."

Suddenly, it seemed, it was March of 1949, and Umphrey Lee had been president of Southern Methodist University for ten years. He could view with some satisfaction the accomplishments of those ten years. Since Umphrey Lee was a man with ideas and the courage to try them out, not every innovation had been successful, but there were few failures and notable successes: SMU had weathered the war years; the major building program was well under way; both the president and his institution were gaining more and more scholarly respect. An encouraging recognition of SMU's place in the educational world came in December of that year when SMU was granted a charter for a chapter of Phi Beta Kappa and Dr. Lee was made the first honorary member of the Southern Methodist University Texas Gamma chapter.

On his tenth anniversary day, 225 members of faculty and staff surprised Dr. and Mrs. Lee with a celebration luncheon. Dr. Herbert Gambrell, who as representative of the faculty had welcomed Umphrey Lee in 1939, reminisced humorously, as did other longtime associates. In more tangible appreciation, six sterling silver goblets were presented to Dr. and Mrs. Lee.

But Dr. Lee had a yearning to teach again. Dean Hosford and Dr. Gambrell, the clever and witty chairman of the department of history, decided that Dr. Lee should also be made professor of history, and they prepared an agreeable and amusing surprise for Dr. Lee and the board of trustees. Dean Hemphill Hosford, presenting a list of proposed new faculty appointments to the Instruction Committee of the board of trustees, in June of 1949, reported in deadpan dialogue: "We have a chance to get a very good fellow to teach eighteenth-century history next fall, without cost. He's a famous scholar. His father was a Methodist minister. He has been to England. He speaks English. . . . His name is . . . U. Lee!"

It was with satisfaction that "Professor of History" Umphrey Lee, after years of administrative duties, made his preparations and once again occupied a professor's chair. In the fall semester, every Monday and Wednesday at 4 p.m. in the seminar room in Dallas Hall he was waiting for the ten men and one woman (an auditor) who had registered for the seminar on "Religion in Eighteenth-Century England." It is probably safe to assume that no one ever had to worry that Dr. Lee might be late. He was always prompt. Professor George C. Baker relates that when university convocations or other meetings were held in McFarlin Auditorium, Dr. Lee was often found sitting alone in the dark shadows backstage waiting for the others who were to be on the stage—ahead of time as usual.

XII

"Dallas' First Citizen"

By 1950, Dr. Lee's reputation was so great that he had the time and energy to satisfy only a small percentage of the requests for his platform appearances. He was in New Orleans to address the Southern Pine Association; was the speaker at the annual Phi Beta Kappa dinner in Dallas; gave his "Clouds Return After the Rain" speech in Chicago; was on the program of the Texas Personnel and Management Association in Austin, Texas; was the principal speaker when Dr. Francis Pendleton Gaines was inaugurated president of Wofford College; and, early in 1953, found time to deliver the Alexander Gustavus Brown Lectures at Randolph-Macon College.

Mrs. Lee accompanied him on these quick trips only occasionally when it was possible to combine a little pleasure with business. When the Southern Association of Schools and Colleges met in Birmingham, Alabama, the Lees decided to drive. Dr. Hosford went along in the Lees' car as did Mrs. John McIntosh, wife of an SMU professor, who took the opportunity to visit one of her children. They spent a leisurely two days on the road each way. All were in a happy frame of mind; it was a gay and relaxing interlude.

President Lee was always at home at SMU to address the first convocation of the semester and regularly crowned the Homecoming Queen at the November Homecoming Football game. In 1953 he had to report to the board of trustees that, in spite of decreasing enrollment, more dormitory space was needed to house the fifty percent of the student body who now came from outside Dallas. Forty-one states, the District of Columbia, and twenty-one foreign countries were now represented at the University.

In the spring, the trustees approved an operating budget of $4,000,000. (The budget for President Lee's first full year at SMU had been less than $800,000.) The trustees also voted to name the planned new student center after Dr. Lee. In the fall of 1952, Lee had turned many internal administrative duties over to Provost Hemphill Hosford to give himself more time for planning the continuing growth of the University, and the next spring, after Dr. Lee's illness, Vice President Willis M. Tate assumed more of the external functions.

In the spring of 1953, Dr. Lee suffered a mild heart attack. It struck one night when he stooped to tie his shoe as he was dressing for the opera. He did not identify the discomfort and, rather than disappoint his hosts, went on to the performance. It was not until two or three weeks later, during his regular physical checkup, that his doctor discovered the condition. He was immediately hospitalized and, in time, seemed to be making a satisfactory recovery. Mrs. Lee, however, began to feel that her husband should make plans to retire from the presidency.

In June, after the heart attack became known, the executive committee of the board of trustees requested that Dr. Lee take a much-needed rest, and that Vice President Tate be charged with general executive responsibilities. Dr. Lee continued to take responsibility for major decisions and kept in close contact with University affairs. When his condition improved he returned to the campus, but adapted a small room on the lower floor of Perkins Administration Building as his office to avoid climbing the steep stairs to the second floor and the suite of rooms occupied by the president and his immediate staff.

In October, one of Dr. Lee's dreams began to come true and on the thirtieth he made what turned out to be his last official public appearance as president of SMU at televised ground-breaking ceremonies of the new Umphrey Lee Student Center. He turned the first shovel of earth as Mrs. Lee and Bishop A. Frank Smith, near at hand, looked on.

Always an opponent of bigotry and discrimination and a true believer in academic freedom as the only way for the universities to help lead to a decent future for all mankind, Umphrey Lee had his courage and his principles tested many times. In 1949, as mentioned in the preceding chapter, Dr. Lee issued a denial that the Fort Worth millionaire had offered SMU a large sum of money if they would bar Jews from admittance. He had added, "However, correspondence has been carried on with Armstrong about his protest against SMU's cooperation with Temple Emanu-El in sponsoring the *Community Course.*"

There had also been protests about SMU's cosponsorship, with President Rainey of the University of Texas and U.S. Senator Morris Sheppard, of the Institute of the National Conference of Christians and Jews.

Before 1939, certain speakers whose viewpoints were considered too radical, controversial, or representative of undesirable religious groups had not been permitted on the campus. Dr. Lee, believing that a university to be a university should present all viewpoints, adopted a liberal policy in regard to campus speakers.

In 1946, the SMU School of Theology set up a small training program for Negroes. Negro ministers in the Dallas area who had an A.B. degree could come to the University twice a week for special noncredit courses. Later they were permitted to audit regular classes without credit. In November 1950, the board of trustees of the University decided to admit Negroes to the Perkins School of Theology as regular students to attend classes and receive credit, and in January 1951, two Dallas Negroes were enrolled. They were victims of an inadequate

173

academic background and were in the school only one semester. They were gone from the school before Dr. Merrimon Cuninggim became dean of the School of Theology in the fall of the same year.

During Dean Cuninggim's first year at SMU, no Negroes were admitted. But preparation was made so that future Negroes admitted to the School of Theology would have an adequate academic background and sufficient adaptability to accept the difficult situation as pioneers in integration. A year later, September 1952, five Negroes were enrolled. In line with the policy of treating all students alike, four of the Negroes asked for and were assigned rooms in the dormitory. The fifth was married and lived in Dallas with his family.

All five of the Negro students participated in Theology School affairs, ate in the Perkins cafeteria, attended chapel, competed in intramural athletics, and attended football games. Through the active cooperation of the Negroes themselves, of Dean Cuninggim, the faculty, other students, and administration, these innovations were anticipated and handled smoothly and unobtrusively.

The first signs of trouble did not crystallize into a serious situation until the following spring when some members of the board of trustees came to think that a mistake had been made and that the Negroes should be removed from the dormitories, possibly even from the University. Some of the Negroes had made friends with their white neighbors and been asked to room with them. There were other minor incidents. The potentially most explosive problem arose when one of the Negroes was invited by a white student to eat in the main University dining hall on Sunday when the Perkins cafeteria was closed. They sat at a table with a group of white students, one of whom was a girl he had already met at a meeting of the Methodist Student Fellowship. The girl was pleased with this new experience, but parents of several students were distressed and began to bring pressure on the administration and the board of trustees. There was a threat of loss of much of the Theology School's support, both financial and otherwise.

It was probably during this period of extreme pressure from within and without the University that Dr. Lee first thought of resigning from the presidency. Dr. Lee was, by nature, a conciliator and not a fighter. Neither was he ever willing to deviate from his principles. If his principles came in conflict with any possible compromise, he was greatly distressed and had no course to follow. He told Bishop Smith at this time that he felt that his health would not permit him to go through the tensions if the situation developed into an open struggle. Concurrent with this problem was the more ferocious and public Beaty affair, a discussion of which follows.

For a time the situation in the School of Theology became most difficult since the three key people, best placed to smooth out difficulties, were temporarily unavailable. Bishop Paul E. Martin, chairman of the trustees' committee of Perkins School of Theology, was overseas; the wife of Bishop A. Frank Smith, chairman of the board of trustees, had suffered a serious heart attack which held him close to Houston; President Lee had suffered a heart attack and was, for a time, unavailable.

The atmosphere was tense during the last part of the spring semester. During the summer respite Dean Cuninggim discussed the problems with the Negro students in person and by letter. The situation was temporarily eased when the Negroes, of their own accord, wrote a letter requesting the housing director not to place them in rooms with white students for the fall semester.

Bishop Martin returned in the fall. By January 1954, the situation had been clarified and resolved. Since that time qualified Negro students have continued to be admitted to the Perkins School of Theology on a non-discriminatory basis. "Perkins School of Theology was evidently the first Methodist institution in North Texas to drop the color bar." [1]

Under Dr. Lee's leadership Negro students were admitted to the Perkins School of Theology. But he did not particularly like the 1954 Supreme Court decision on the racial question. Law by fiat of the Supreme Court rather than by legislation, enforced segregation, or enforced integration, all seemed wrong to him. Dr. Lee was a "committed gradualist" in race relations. He was also a realist, and when he saw no prospect of returning to slow, easy changes, and feared rebellion, he moved to place his influence with those trying to work for a peaceful solution. He was one of the nearly 300 Protestant ministers signing an appeal urging respect for and compliance with the law. At the request of Robert G. Storey, dean of the School of Law at SMU, he became a member of the Civil Rights Advisory Committee of North Texas and had attended the first meeting before his death.

By 1951, pressure groups were becoming more of a problem in the United States and to Southern Methodist University. Dr. Lee reported to the trustees in November that some self-appointed committee had asked him to send, for their approval, copies of all the texts used in one of the schools at the University. "Since I could not think up a reasonably polite answer, I simply did not respond at all. . . . A university must maintain its integrity and the rights of its own governing board. . . . This is not a fashion show or a vaudeville act where the worth of the goods is to be determined by the way the audience happens to be feeling at a particular moment," wrote Dr. Lee, in his Report to the Board of Trustees, November 15, 1951.

By 1953, the United States was in the throes of McCarthyism. It was the heyday of the communist witch hunt and near hysteria in the country out of fear of imminent internal communist take-over. Eventually the repercussions reached the

[1] Walter N. Vernon, *Methodism Moves Across North Texas*, p. 351.

Southwest. Dr. John O. Beaty, a longtime faculty member and chairman of the department of English at SMU, returned from World War II years with the United States Intelligence Service to write a book, *The Iron Curtain over America*, reported to be an exposé of communist activities in the United States.

The publication of that book ushered in two of the most disquieting years of Umphrey Lee's life. In reality, the publication of *The Iron Curtain over America* had not come as a complete surprise either to Dr. Lee or to the Southern Methodist University Press, publishers of the *Southwest Review*. In early spring of 1951, or before, the Press had heard that Dr. Beaty was seeking a publisher for a book, reportedly anti-Jewish, and the director of the Press was asked what the SMU Press would do "if it had submitted to it a book manuscript which expressed a thesis which was obviously in conflict with and counter to the basis upon which SMU and the Methodist Church were founded and operated." Director Allen Maxwell replied that they would not touch it.

The thesis of the book, it appeared, was that Jews, or Khazars, are responsible for many of the woes of the world. Dr. Beaty continued to insist through the controversy that he was not anti-Semitic but anticommunist, pro-Christian, and pro-American. There appeared to be a fine distinction in his semantics between the Khazars who were not Semites but had embraced Judaism in the eighth or ninth century A.D., and the Jews who were true Semites. The anti-Christian, anti-American, procommunist conspiracy he attributed to the Khazars. Most American Jews were Khazars, he believed, and his examples of people or organizations fostering the communist conspiracy, particularly at the Dallas level, emphasized the Jews. Presumably these were Khazars and not true Semites. Some of the criticism of the Beaty book's thesis centered on his quibbling about the definition of "Semitic" and questioned that Khazars existed in sufficient numbers to be a force in any conspiracy.

The SMU Press and Dr. Lee were much disturbed that such a book, if published, carrying the author's identification as a Southern Methodist University professor and chairman of the department of English, would appear to have the tacit sanction of the University. Fears were somewhat dispelled when Dr. Beaty decided to publish the book privately through a Dallas printing company, making a large circulation unlikely. But Dr. Beaty had connections they did not suspect, such as Gerald L. K. Smith, leader of the Christian National Crusade, Hollywood gossip columnist Hedda Hopper, Lt. General George E. Stratemeyer, and others. The import of the book was such that by the autumn of 1953, *The Iron Curtain over America* was said to have gone through nine printings totaling 45,000 copies. SMU's approval was extravagantly implied.[2]

Meanwhile, the University Press, using the positive approach, had hurried publication of a volume representative of SMU's position: a book of essays, *Medicine for a Sick World: Essays and Reflections,* by David Lefkowitz, Rabbi Emeritus of Temple Emanu-El, for which Umphrey Lee had written the foreword; and in the summer issue of the *Southwest Review,* an article by Mrs. Margaret Hartley, then assistant editor, "The Subliterature of Hate in America," designed, without mentioning Beaty or his book, to show that such ideas as his were not "indicative, at least of the institution's intellectual climate."

In February of 1953, Dr. Lee spoke to the Dallas Salesmanship Club. Without mentioning Beaty specifically, he said, "I do not know how to put the matter any stronger than in the words of the supreme legislative body of my church: 'anti-

[2] *Time,* March 5, 1952; *The Campus,* November 18, 1953; Letter from General Stratemeyer in President's files; "Statement of Activities from SMU Press in Relation to John O. Beaty," Allen Maxwell, Director, April 5, 1954.

Semitism is a deadly sin,' and so are anti-Catholicism and anti-Protestantism. From all such sins, Good Lord, deliver us!"

A subsequent book by Ralph Lord Roy, *Apostles of Discord,* devoted eight pages to Beaty and his controversial 437-page book, which Roy considered "the most extensive piece of anti-Semitic literature in the history of America's racist movement." The Rev. Ralph Lord Roy was a Methodist clergyman and a graduate student at Union Theological Seminary and Columbia University in New York City.

The autumn 1953 issue of the *Southwest Review* included an essay-review of *Apostles of Discord* by Mrs. Hartley, entitled "The Protestant Underworld." It devoted three paragraphs of the five-page review to Roy's discussion of the Beaty book and mentioned laudatory notices of the book in such journals as Gerald L. K. Smith's *The Cross and the Flag* as well as unfavorable comments in such publications as the Methodist *Zions Herald.*

Dr. Beaty reacted at once in defense of his thesis of immediate communist danger in the United States and serious infiltration of subversive elements at SMU. So began a series of vicious attacks on the University that created national attention and lasted through the school year. Many people, including Mrs. Lee, believed that these attacks contributed to Dr. Lee's declining health and eventual resignation from the presidency for health reasons. The mental and emotional strain of fighting for the University that was so much a part of himself came at a time when he was trying to recover from the heart attack.

Dr. Beaty's next action was a surprise and a shock to Dr. Lee. Early in 1954 Beaty directly attacked his critics and SMU with a pamphlet entitled "How to Capture a University." The pamphlet said that non-Christian elements were making an effort to dominate SMU; that the *Southwest Review* was one of several University activities which had been infiltrated; that at SMU those hostile to Christian civilization were concen-

trating upon the publishing interests, upon its preacher training, and upon its book-selling agency, as well as its public
lectures.

The pamphlet attacked the *Community Course,* joint effort
of SMU and Temple Emanu-El; labeled the activities of the
National Conference of Christians and Jews as brainwashing
and asked, "Can you guess who does the brainwashing?" It
condemned the *Southwest Review* for its use of John Rosenfield, amusements editor of the *Dallas Morning News,* as a
reviewer of books and plays; condemned the bookstore for
selling a book by Frederick Engels, *The British Labour Movement,* which happened to have a list of V. I. Lenin's works
on the back of the jacket.

"How to Capture a University" carried a conglomerate
photostat purporting to show the non-Christian and leftist slant
of the *Southwest Review.* Included were small segments of:
a John Rosenfield essay; an article by Stanley Marcus, president
of Neiman-Marcus, "Are American Businessmen Moral
Eunuchs?" an article by Henry M. Wriston, president of Brown
University; a sentence mentioning Stanley Marcus as spokesman for the sponsoring committee of the "freedom festival";
a mention of the B'nai B'rith friendship awards (of $50 and
$25) to the Perkins theology students for contributions in
the area of social ethics; announcement of the summer workshop of the NCCJ; and the Engels book jacket.

Dr. Beaty admitted to the investigating committee of the
board of trustees that he financed the publishing and mailing
of the pamphlets to the administrators of SMU, to those who
were attacked in the articles, and to the people to whom he
had mailed copies of *The Iron Curtain over America.* A later
mailing of approximately 3,000 copies of "How to Capture a
University" went to parents of SMU students, names and
addresses taken from the school directory and financed by
another source. Dr. Beaty stated that this mailing was effected

after Dr. Lee had turned the matter over to the trustees.

For months local newspapers were flooded with letters to the editor both for and against Dr. Beaty. The Public Affairs Luncheon Club passed and sent to the SMU board of trustees, the president, and the dean of the School of Theology a resolution condemning the policy of "sponsoring such self-styled liberals" as Richard H. Rovere, Henry Wriston, and Ralph Lord Roy by allowing them to speak on the campus. Roy was scheduled to speak at Perkins School of Theology by invitation of the Student Council and the Dallas Council of Churches.

On February 10, 1954, *The Campus* urged the administration to take a stand since Dr. Beaty kept insisting that only "junior" faculty and staff members had repudiated his book. After the publication of Beaty's book, Lon Tinkle, professor of French, who could hardly be called a junior member of the SMU faculty, characterized *The Iron Curtain over America* as the worst book of 1952 in his column in the *Dallas Morning News* book page and, in a later column, had disposed of Hollywood columnist Hedda Hopper's praise of the book, writing, "What she knows about international affairs can be inscribed on the head of a pin."

A day or two after the article in *The Campus* asked the University to take a stand, an announcement came from the president's office that Dr. Lee was out of the city and no statement would be made by the administration until his return.

On February 16, the SMU faculty, in a regularly scheduled meeting, publicly repudiated the Beaty pamphlet by a vote of 114 to 2. Dr. Beaty complained that he had not had a chance to be there and defend himself. He admitted that he had received notice of the regular meeting but had chosen not to attend. He claimed that the action of the faculty was a big surprise to him.

Seven prominent Dallas Protestant ministers wrote to Dr.

Lee expressing "outraged Christian conscience over Beaty's inflammatory and divisive writings," and a group of SMU law professors denounced Beaty's book as a collection of "spurious doctrines and bigoted theories of racist and religious prejudice." [3] The Board of World Peace of The Methodist Church, Ralph W. Sockman, president, sent a supporting letter to SMU, and the Perkins theologs applauded the faculty action and begged for freedom of expression for all pro- and anti-Beaty supporters.

Dr. Beaty had claimed that the SMU bookstore had refused to sell his book. The manager offered to reorder for anyone who wanted the book. He explained later to the investigating committee that the policy of the store had been, and was, to stock a few copies, six to ten, of any professor's new book, as a courtesy, but after that to order on request—a procedure that had been followed by the store with Dr. Beaty.

Time had called Dr. Lee "Dallas' First Citizen," and in their April 12, 1954 issue, traced the whole Beaty controversy in a manner distinctly favorable to SMU and to Dr. Lee.

This was not the first time that Umphrey Lee had found himself involved with the author of "How to Capture a University." Dr. Beaty had long been a self-appointed guardian of SMU's moral, political, and religious climate. As early as the 1930's Beaty had decided that Henry Nash Smith, one of SMU's brilliant young professors, was an undesirable influence at the University. He was determined to implement his departure because Smith had dared to write the introduction to a novelette by William Faulkner, *Miss Zilphia Gant*. Working behind the scenes through Bishop John M. Moore, Dr. Lee, then pastor of Highland Park Methodist Church, was able to help retain Smith at the University. Bishop Hiram A. Boaz was chairman of the Morals Committee of the board of trustees that censured Beaty for "unduly" circulating a letter com-

[3] *Time,* April 12, 1954; *Dallas Times Herald,* February 25, 1954.

182

plaining about the "lax attitude of certain faculty members toward the moral standards of SMU" and declared the complaints without foundation.[4] Henry Nash Smith later left SMU of his own accord and went on to become a distinguished professor, the author of scholarly books, an authority on Mark Twain, and the editor of the great collection of Mark Twain material bequeathed to the University of California by Twain's daughter.

When Dr. Beaty returned from the army in 1947, he eliminated "Awake and Sing" from the freshman English required reading list at SMU. The author, Clifford Odets, "was a communist and he was also Jewish"; and the work was published by a Jewish publishing house and praised by a Jewish paper! [5] He attacked *The American Way of Life* by Barnes and Reudi, a textbook dealing with American social and political problems then being used in one of the social science courses. In Dr. Beaty's opinion it contained Red propaganda. He lodged a protest when the theater department staged a performance of the popular play, "The Man Who Came to Dinner."

The Campus and the Dallas Jewish community continued to press for the administration of the University to take some action on the then current Beaty controversy. Dallas Jews, many of whom had been loyal supporters of the University, felt that Dr. Beaty should be jettisoned. Another opinion was that the dismissal of Beaty would be a disavowal of SMU's policy of academic freedom. About this time someone, without Dr. Lee's knowledge, inquired of the committee dealing with academic freedom and tenure of the American Association of University Professors, local chapter, whether or not expressed anti-Semitism would be sufficient grounds in their eyes for dismissal of a college professor with tenure. The reply

[4] *Dallas Journal,* January 26, 1933.
[5] Transcript of the hearing conducted by a committee of the board of trustees.

was that it would not. Academic freedom, they said, had to apply both ways. Dismissal might result in AAUP blacklisting that would do irreparable damage to SMU. All this was duly reported to Dr. Lee.

Meantime Dr. Lee hesitated. He felt that the handling of this problem had to rest on his shoulders alone. Other members of the administration were kept silent. No public statement was forthcoming between the time of Dr. Lee's strong enunciation of his church's stand on anti-Semitism before the Salesmanship Club in February 1953, and the 1954 release to the press that he had referred the eight-page pamphlet, "How to Capture a University" to the board of trustees. In that press release Dr. Lee stated that he desired publicly and gladly to take full responsibility for the cordial relations between SMU, Temple Emanu-El, and B'nai B'rith, and accepted full responsibility for the cooperation of the University with Catholic, Protestant, and Jewish leaders in the National Conference of Christians and Jews. He thanked Dallas citizens who had provided, under the chairmanship of Mr. Stanley Marcus, the so-called "Freedom Lecture" series of the year before.

A special committee from the board of trustees was appointed to investigate the allegations made in the pamphlet. Chairman D. A. Hulcy, S. J. Hay, Dr. W. W. Ward, J. S. Bridwell, James Willson, and Floyd James attended one or both of the two days of hearings conducted April 5 and April 12, 1954, interviewed Dr. Beaty and other people most intimately involved, and examined the various documents.

Dr. Beaty's attitude seemed to be that he was saving the University from itself; that, while the administration and the board of trustees were busy with other things, the communists and other non-Christians had infiltrated the University; and that, since no word of any kind was heard from the administration up to the time of Lee's statement to the Salesmanship Club (Beaty did not consider himself anti-Semitic) , he assumed even after that that the University approved of his effort to cleanse it of subversive elements.

At its May meeting the board of trustees adopted the report of the investigating committee. Dr. Beaty was reprimanded for releasing his pamphlet directly to the press via *The Campus,* the public, and the patrons, instead of complaining through the proper channels at the University—his dean, the provost, and the president. Neither had he protested to the *Southwest Review.* The board of trustees concluded that facts did not bear out the allegations made by Beaty in the pamphlet. The trustees also issued the statement, "All persons who find themselves out of harmony with these principles [of Christian education as set down by President Charles C. Selecman in 1938] and unable to support these ideals ought to retire from the University, and no teaching is tolerated which is in conflict with Christian principles." [6]

Dr. Beaty chose to interpret the statement as being directed at the "non-Christian" elements at SMU and said that so far as he could see nothing hostile to him was in the action of the board of trustees. Consequently, he did not resign. When Dr. Willis M. Tate became president of the University, however, he immediately gave Dr. Beaty to understand that the statement of the trustees was in fact directed at him. Thereafter, although Beaty continued to teach until the time of his regular retirement, he issued no more publications and no more statements. With the repudiation of Senator McCarthy and the reaction against his tenets, the attacks on Southern Methodist University decreased gradually and the principle of academic freedom continued to be upheld.

It is, of course, impossible to evaluate Dr. Lee's handling of the Beaty problem. Many of his most loyal supporters felt that more forceful action on his part would have prevented its reaching crisis proportions. They felt that this was an ex-

[6] *The Campus,* May 19, 1954; Report of the board of trustees.

ample of Dr. Lee's great reluctance to do anything to hurt another person, an admirable trait, yet a magnanimity that limited his effectiveness as an administrator. Someone has said that the defects of great men reclaim them to humanity— inevitably there are defects. So it was with Umphrey Lee— a virtue, carried to excess, became the defect that reclaimed him to humanity.

As the Beaty affair progressed to a climax, Dr. Lee's own personal and professional crisis had been developing. During the summer months he had attempted, with rest and relaxation, to recapture his former vigor. Seemingly he was returning to health, and the fall semester of the 1953-54 session began auspiciously. On Friday, September 18, Dr. and Mrs. Lee gave their usual tea in Fondren Library, honoring new students.

In October, Mrs. Lee welcomed the wives of new and old faculty at the traditional coffee in the president's home. Dr. Lee continued to spend much time resting, but it was reported to the executive committee of the board of trustees at their October meeting that he was getting along fine and would return to their meetings soon. In November, the members of the board of trustees began to gather in Dallas for their fall meeting, all anxious about the health of their President Umphrey Lee. The chairman of the Board made a happy ceremony of presenting the returned Dr. Lee to his accustomed place when the first session convened.

But Dr. Lee's doctor still did not believe that he should begin full-time activities and, early in the spring, the difficult decision was finally made—Umphrey Lee would resign from the presidency of Southern Methodist University. In a poignant letter, dated March 11 and written to the chairman of the board of trustees, Bishop A. Frank Smith, President Lee explained that he could not in good conscience continue holding an office in which he was physically unable to function on a full-time basis. With his usual succinct phraseology he

186

wrote, "The presidency of the University is not a part-time job." He asked Bishop Smith, "my longtime friend, to submit my resignation to the Board of Trustees of Southern Methodist University."

At a special meeting on March 30, the letter was presented to the board of trustees. The state of Dr. Lee's health gave no alternative but to accept his resignation. Judge J. E. Hickman immediately moved that Dr. Lee be named chancellor without administrative duties but with ex officio membership on the executive committee of the board of trustees. The members were eager for Dr. Lee to remain in an advisory capacity, for "his insight, judgment and spirit will be more than sufficient to make him invaluable."

In his usual humorous self-deprecating way Dr. Lee recounted that he had asked Bishop Smith what a chancellor was supposed to do, and that the Bishop had replied, "Just walk across the campus occasionally and try to look benevolent."

Dr. Lee was to remain as chancellor until the University's normal retirement time at age 65 in 1958 when the position of chancellor would cease to exist. The problem of selecting a new president was then taken up, and Bishop Paul E. Martin was appointed to head a committee to nominate a successor to Dr. Lee at the regular May 6 meeting of the Board.

Dr. Lee resigned the presidency just a few days before his sixty-first birthday on March 23, having given Southern Methodist University for fifteen years an administration characterized by good taste, common sense, and devotion to improving the intellectual climate of the University. The public reaction to his resignation was a mixture of regret, gratitude for his contribution, and concern over the state of his health. Friends, faculty, and staff invented ways to show their affection and appreciation. The night before his birthday more than 700 students gathered outside the president's home on Marquette to serenade the Lees. Umphrey and Mary Lee stood between the white pillars of the porch to greet the group. Dr. Lee smilingly accepted the three-tiered birthday cake and bronze plaque presented by Bill Brice, president of the Student Council.

The Campus reported that Mrs. Lee, attractive in a "smart white dress," graciously and charmingly told the students that she and Dr. Lee were thrilled by the visit. At first they had been afraid that the neighborhood boys and dogs might get in the way. She complimented the cake, decorated in the University colors: SMU in blue letters, HAPPY BIRTHDAY in red, and fifteen red candles, the last two of which Dr. Lee blew out to the accompaniment of "Happy Birthday," followed by "Varsity," "For He's a Jolly Good Fellow," and "Auld Lang Syne" under the direction of Don Barnes of the Student Council. The bronze plaque read:

> To you, President Umphrey Lee:
> We who have studied under your inspiring leadership bring our profound thanks for the brave new world of brotherhood you gave us at our alma mater and yours, SMU.

Umphrey Lee had been president of SMU for fifteen years and one month, a tenure only four months less than that of Dr. Selecman, the longest up to that time. He could feel that the University had progressed far along the path he envisioned. The faculty now numbered 200 full-time faculty members, and the University's worth was $29,000,000. On the 150-acre campus were fifty permanent buildings and a football stadium. In Dr. Lee's last year, 1381 contributors had shown their confidence in SMU by subscribing $303,750 to the Sustentation Fund. But Dr. Lee's greatest satisfaction could spring from knowing that the University's academic stature had been enhanced, the student body more selective and less provincial (one out of five students now came from outside Texas), and the curriculum broader based along lines Dr. Lee had sketched in the early years of his presidency.

There were still many problems to be solved: enrollment had to wait for the crop of war babies to reach college age; the University was the center of controversy as a result of the Beaty situation and "McCarthy" aspect of the times; and the critical money shortage continued. Students, faculty, Dallas businessmen, and other SMU supporters engaged in active dialogue regarding a man to take over what Umphrey Lee had so far advanced. An editorial in *The Campus,* March 17, 1954, headed "New President Needs Courage," listed problems facing the University and urged a new president who would continue to defend academic freedom.

The board of trustees met for its regular semi-annual meeting on May 6. The first order of business was to send a message of affection to the Lees and express the hope that Dr. Lee would continue to improve. They then heard the report of the nominating committee and elected Dr. Willis M. Tate to the presidency of Southern Methodist University, a choice that was acceptable, also, to Dr. Lee, who felt that Dr. Tate had been most effective in all phases of the University. Dr. Lee was confident that his dream of a great future for Southern Methodist University was shared by the new president.

XIII

"As I See It"

The four years between his resignation from the presidency of Southern Methodist University until his death must have been for Dr. Lee in many ways a full and rewarding period. It was less strenuous and less spectacular. Virtually freed from routine responsibility, he could devote his time to his ever-engrossing research, reading, and writing. As chancellor he kept his small office on the first floor of Perkins Administration Building and, in a small secluded study of the third floor of Fondren Library, filled with his books, he prepared his addresses; completed *A Short History of Methodism* with Dr. William Warren Sweet; wrote the booklet "For the Rising Generation"; worked on his last book, *Our Fathers and Us;* and composed his weekly newspaper column.

From September 1956 until his death in 1958, Dr. Lee wrote a delightful and popular column for the *Dallas Times Herald,* "As I See It," which illustrated the high degree of similarity between his writing and speaking styles. His style as a columnist was sophisticated or, sometimes, reminiscent of Will Rogers in his use of the folksy anecdote to illustrate his commentary which might be on: world affairs; old age; the folk ways of Texans; preachers; kilts; oratory; semantically minded little old ladies; Cicero; Ogden Nash; or politics. Whether urbane or folksy, his style was always appropriate to his subject and illustrative of his viewpoint on a particular issue. These articles have a vitality, a zest, and a self-revealing absence of earlier restraints that fascinates. A friend once asked if he usually knew the answers in crossword puzzles and quiz games. He replied, "Yes, you see, words are my business."

Umphrey Lee was a historian. History and religion dominated his life. Some of his friends have speculated that, if he had not been brought up in the family of a dedicated minister, he might have adopted history as a career. He was convinced that the past as history is essential to an understanding of the present, and his approach to any subject was that of the historian.

Any conclusion had to be, to Dr. Lee, historically plausible. This is evident in all his writing. He frequently filled in with discussions of political, social, and economic aspects of the period in which a man lived or the particular doctrine had its beginning. He was adept at the thumb-nail sketch of a past period, carrying both the fact and the flavor of the time.

But history and religion were so tightly interwoven in everything Dr. Lee composed that one cannot doubt either his devotion to Christianity or his infatuation with history. He had an intellectual knowledge of the philosophers, but he was more historian than philosopher. Although born in the last decade of the nineteenth century Dr. Lee was not a nineteenth-century man. His son, as mentioned before, identified him as a post-Victorian; others would say that he was post-post-Victorian. Some of the taboos and restraints of the earlier period remained. He could not bring himself to speak openly of sex but wrote somewhat vaguely of our "animal instincts." Favorite authors were not the "moderns." He had read and understood "The Wasteland" by T. S. Eliot, but he did not particularly like it. He much preferred Robert Frost, Edna St. Vincent Millay, and George Bernard Shaw.

However, in many ways Umphrey Lee made the transition to the twentieth century without undue difficulty and even in the 1940's anticipated many of the problems that plague the United States in the 1970's. He may not have discerned the full significance of changes going on in the world and in the mind of man, but there is ample evidence that he came close to sensing the flavor and fever of the new century. He also enlarged the view of the possibilities of the future and was an optimist about Western civilization. Reading Spengler did not change his mind.

In his sermons, Dr. Lee quoted others and did not force his own theological views on his hearers, but his sermons express the sparkle and vitality of a man who has come to terms with life and death. In his scholarly addresses, frequently to students and educators, he adhered closely to the facts of history and pointed logical conclusions; but, in speaking to other groups on the current scene or in his column, "As I See It," his own opinions stand out sharply and distinctly, stated with clarity and succinctness. The newspaper medium gave full range to his talent for social criticism, often with a gentle, ironical, humorous touch.

Dr. Lee was a shrewd observer of the national scene. In 1946, he spoke of a "world becoming increasingly political" and noted "this strain between stability and change." (*Render unto the People,* pp. 130 and 146.) In the same series of lectures he observed: "The country is becoming secular with almost geometrical progression. . . . Men once gave themselves consciously or unconsciously, to their homes and their towns and their churches. For men cannot live without community. When the old cords are broken, there must be new ones." (*Render unto the People,* pp. 52 and 158.)

He felt that our national cleavages were "more serious than those which this nation has known since the days of slavery"; that "this strain between stability and change" was due to: the "divisive forces" in our society; "the passionate character of our politics"; "the centralization of government until it offers unwanted opportunities for control"; and to the passing of the emphasis upon religion in the lives of the people. He

192

pointed out that "a new world has brought new problems, and our old conceptions must be reconsidered." (*Render unto the People,* pp. 39-138.)

The growth of population and wealth, the movement into the cities, the increasing complexity of modern business, radio, and television all came under scrutiny. In one radio address concerning the world's advanced communication technologies and man's subsequent anxiety, Dr. Lee illustrated:

I asked my son how it feels to jump from an airplane. I wanted to know if the parachutist has a great sense of falling. He said, "No, he seems to be floating." I asked, "Why doesn't he feel that he is falling?" "Well," said my boy, "You know he isn't passing anything."

We are passing too much. It would be remarkable if any man could keep his feeling of security in a world where the scene changes rapidly. I am sure the new way is better. But I am not sure it is easier on us. Every time Mr. Molotov mutters in his whiskers Grandfather gets down his squirrel rifle. . . .

Quite seriously, we must take into account the shock to our nervous systems that is caused by our constantly keeping our ears to the keyhole of the world. . . . Part of the advantages of our fathers lay in the time lag between the occurrence of existing events and the reporting of them to the people. . . . There is not quite the urgency about things that happened in Washington last month as about what happened yesterday or today. ("The Community of the Confident.")

In his opinion the old country store had a valuable function as a discussion and debating society. Each bit of news was masticated thoroughly, avoiding "intellectual indigestion," and although our forefathers knew less than the current generation, "they may have understood more of what they did know." (*Render unto the People,* pp. 44-45.) He saw World War II as the failure to solve the fundamental moral problems that

193

came out of having to live together and thought it was inevitable in the kind of world we had. "Black eyes have no monetary value so far as I know, but men and boys will continue to accummulate them. Men fight in spite of the economic motives that should prevent them." ("As I See It," December 9, 1956.) "In one generation we have had two wars and nobody wins." ("As I See It," August 18, 1957.)

Speaking at the memorial services for the 127 former SMU students who died in World War II, Dr. Lee looked hopefully to the future, saying that their sacrifices had assured that we do not have to go back to the jungle but have extended time and a new option on a world where we can find "justice and peace."

Dr. Lee once noted that the Vice President of the United States had been stoned and that the American flag had been torn down in Venezuela, and that the Democrats blamed Mr. Nixon while the Republicans, not yet heard from, would probably find it to be Mr. Truman's fault.

But the fault is not basically that of Mr. Nixon. We are not popular in South America, . . . Europe, Asia, Africa, the Near East and the Far East. . . . There was a time in our history when we were widely popular: that was when we were a small struggling nation. . . . Everybody loves you when you are poor and helpless. It may be that no one will lend you money, but everybody is kind and sympathetic. . . . So long as we are big and reasonably prosperous we shall not have too many friends . . . no matter who is our ambassador. ("As I See It," May 18, 1958.)

In one column where Dr. Lee explored the many theories advanced as the reasons Custer lost to the Sioux at the Little Big Horn, his conclusion was: "Too many Indians." He philosophized further on diplomacy and other nations, saying that our allies fear us because we are too self-righteous, too inflexible; that our diplomatic approach ought to assume that other people can be intelligent sometimes and even honest. "The Indians never trusted us, and they had good reason. If a people assume that they are always right, they must be sure that they are always right on the battlefield. If we are never wrong in diplomacy, we must never be wrong in battle. And sometimes there may be too many Indians." ("As I See It," March 23, 1958.)

Earlier Dr. Lee had written that "the prerequisite of international peace is the opening of doors in the closed minds of our people. We who cannot imagine any good thing that isn't made in America are hopeless from the standpoint of the peacemaker." (*Jesus the Pioneer*, p. 16.) An awareness of the atavistic nature of man's "stranger hatred" is illustrated by the following story:

Many years ago, I was on the top of a bus in Scotland. It was a year when we were wearing bell-bottomed trousers. I looked around indignantly to see two boys looking at my pants legs and rolling in merriment. They were wearing kilts.

So our history confines us. The foreigner is strange. Oftentimes he can't even speak English. Of course, you can't trust him. . . . But the things that really irritate are the kilts and the bell-bottomed trousers. ("As I See It," June 23, 1957.)

Perhaps he was hopeful about international understanding, but he wrote, "I have never been for world government because I think it is too far in the future." (Letter to X. Carson.)

The bulk of Dr. Lee's rhetoric places an emphasis on the interrelation of education, religion, and government or, more specifically, their confrontation. A previous chapter (the ninth) discusses Dr. Lee's distress over the loss of direct and indirect religious teaching in the schools. As he saw it, in a public welfare state the church and state are concerned in the same areas of human life. There is danger of a collision, and the old concept of separation of church and state must be reconsidered. "To say that the church must not touch on areas controlled by the state is going to be difficult in a time when man is born in a government hospital, introduced into the world by a doctor on the government payroll, educated by the state, employed under circumstances and terms dictated by law, retired on a government pension, buried by government insurance, and mourned by a widow supported by social security." (*Render unto the People,* pp. 117-20.)

How can the Protestant religion live fully in "our kind of democracy" without losing prized liberty or even losing the religion it professes, particularly in a secular state where many in the population are indifferent to religion and may go so far as to object to the moral standards of the church? These thoughts were expressed in 1946 when there had been no Supreme Court decision on prayer in the public schools. At this time no state excluded Bible reading by law, and eleven states had statutes requiring Bible reading. Dr. Lee made it clear that he did not believe in forcing children of one faith to participate in religious exercises which would offend or deny their own inheritance. (*Render unto the People,* pp. 9-39.)

In "The City of Cain" Dr. Lee had discussed the social and religious implications in the changes from an agrarian to an urban society and explored one of his favorite subjects— religion as related to the sociological aspects of the times. He mentioned the fear of the complex and the new; strange inventions; intensification of human problems in great populations; moral difficulties; and the effect of our changed method of life upon the opportunity for religious work—all contributing to distrust of the city. (*Jesus the Pioneer,* pp. 24-25.) But he reminded his readers that "the Christian ethic is the ethic of cities, of people living together in an urbanized world," for it arose in the crowded districts of Mediterranean cities. ("The Spiritual Basis of Democracy," p. 94.)

Although Dr. Lee showed concern over the future role of the church in social action, he believed "that one of the church's primary ministries in any field is to promote worship," and another primary service of the church "is to give men some orientation that will put the affairs of life into perspective." (*Render unto the People,* p. 131). He criticized belief in the myth that human events naturally and irresistibly move toward some significant utopian end; deplored the passion for great churches and the creation of bureaucratic controls in churches, developments that do not always help to promote fellowship and brotherhood. He censured the Protestant churches for their failure to reach unanimity among themselves regarding the social problems of marriage, divorce, education, and justice in our economic life; he blamed the churches for doing so little to relieve racial tensions: "Christianity was—let us hope also is—a living religion, not an aggregate of disparate beliefs. . . . A very respectable part of the Christian world believes that Christianity teaches a regard for human personality which is not satisfied with the saving of a soul in a future paradise but demands the release of human potentialities here." ("The Spiritual Basis of Democracy.")

The effect of social change upon religion, government, and education formed much of the rhetoric of Dr. Lee, particularly in his later years. He became one of the Southwest's most literate spokesmen of the moderate viewpoint. He once wrote, "In many ways the Bible is a slow motion picture of social change." (*The Bible and Business,* p. 160.) He felt that the aspects of transition in the eighteenth century facilitated the early Methodist movement and was deeply concerned about the adverse effect of rapid social change in the twentieth century upon the modern Methodist Church—in fact, upon religion in general. While he evinced concern for the lack of religious emphasis in our time and voiced some fear for the church in an era of change, he presented his characteristically balanced viewpoint when he maintained: "There is no denying that both stability and change are essential to the social order if it is to relate itself to man's needs," and if our society becomes inflexibly dedicated to preserving the status quo, "sterility will displace creativeness." (*Render unto the People,* pp. 142-43.)

In *Render unto the People,* a collection of the Cole Lectures which he delivered in the School of Religion at Vanderbilt University in 1946, and in the posthumously published *Our Fathers and Us,* Dr. Lee examined in detail the complexities of the structural shift in religion's place in our governmental system. Aristotle insisted that man is essentially a "political animal." Lee constantly attempted to convince that religion most have a part in life. He did not hesitate to speak forcefully on secular problems, the place of Christianity in a democracy in the process of change, and the confrontation of church and state. In the Cole Lectures he described Americans as "a people being taught rapidly to believe that there are no goods save those of material things, to be gained largely through political means," and as a people who "are being welded together with a passion, continuous and bitter." (*Render unto the People,* p. 53.) For ours is an age in which "political and economic opinions are held with all the passion formerly associated with theology":

As the state controls more and more of the interests which formerly were left to individuals and to voluntary associations, it is inevitable that the church and state should confront each other in a manner which would have seemed strange to our forefathers (pp. 117-18).

What could be done if a secular majority decided that organized religion were dangerous to the peace and safety of the commonwealth seems to me plain enough (p. 21).

And it would be well to keep in mind that it is not necessary to outlaw Christian teaching to destroy the church (p. 21).

History does not encourage the hope that church groups will not succumb to the temptation to adopt very worldly methods in political strife (p. 129).

We are in the midst of a secular stream which is not destroying religion but simply leaving it behind (p. 52).

Accepting the imperfections of our world, Dr. Lee felt that the social ends of Christianity had the most favorable climate for achievement in a democracy, but he stressed the efficacy of patience in our quest toward the perfect society:

It is one of the ironies of history that the doctrine of evolution, which presumably taught that life has evolved through untold millions of years, should have encouraged men to believe that an ideal society could be achieved in a few decades. . . . The faith which the people of the world have put in the coming of the millennium by legislation is one of the saddening phases of recent Western history (p. 50).

Dr. Lee often spoke of the complexities of modern life. He felt there was need for more organization in the Protestant church in a complex, industrialized, computerized society, that the early Christians might be emulated to advantage by their modern counterparts. The early Christians functioned in a hostile society as does the modern church, in many respects. Lee spoke of a need for a greater appreciation of the corporate life of Christianity. He noted that "the early Christians pooled their resources," and the early Christian churches "were actually labor unions in that religion was an integral part

199

of their daily economic struggle." (*The Bible and Business,* p. 152.)

On occasions, he could speak of religion and the church with the succinctness and candor which he usually reserved for other matters. He entertained doubts as to the value of the "eager and voluble prophet in the pulpit" and declared: "The price of liberty in religion, as elsewhere, is that we must sometimes suffer fools until we can decide whether they are fools or prophets." (*Render unto the People,* pp. 137 and 131.) In his newspaper column some years later he wrote: "The danger of religious fanatics has always been that they think God is on their side." ("As I See It," August 18, 1957.)

Dr. Lee believed that the church has a prophetic mission, but he held overzealous pulpit exhortation in low regard. Far too many preachers, "unburdened by knowledge and uninhibited by breadth of experience have berated their charges," for denunciation is easier than constructive labor in investing meaning to religion in a modern secular world. In *Render unto the People* he synthesized his feelings on this matter more than once:

Happy is the church whose leaders have courage equal to their convictions and intelligence equal to their courage (p. 138).

I have insisted upon the freedom of the church and of the pulpit. It is a hard doctrine, for prophets are few and fools are many (p. 156).

The church is also a conserver of values. There are priests as well as prophets. . . . But the institution preserves even if it sometimes embalms (pp. 156-57).

Christians came in for their share of bold criticism. Lee did not absolve them from responsibility for facing the unique problems of the twentieth century. He had begun early to reiterate that Christians must mature and support their faith aggressively and intelligently if the church was not to pass away. One of his sermons, "Saints Wanted," in the 1930's, published in *The Southwestern Advocate,* speaks directly:

I incline to think that, so far as our troubled world is concerned, the greatest thing that could happen would be for some of the "babes in Christ" to grow up. . . . Certainly when times are as difficult as they are now . . . the Church needs mature Christians. . . .

How many church members have progressed beyond a childish attitude toward the church itself? Is the preacher interesting? Is the choir tolerable? Are the church members friendly? Now, these are not matters to be neglected. No preacher has a license to be dull. No choir need be unduly painful. Church members should be given to hospitality at church as well as at home. But even a child in Christ ought not to hang his Christian life on such matters as these. . . .

For this reason many churches waste their strength coddling their members. Instead of being an army of the living God, they are simply divisions of a spiritual nursery. Ministers and officials have little time for extending the tents of Israel, for they are kept busy chucking religious babes under their spiritual chins to keep them amused. So-and-so must be kept in good humor. Here is no sense of the awfulness of man's relation to the Eternal God. Here is no realization that the church is an opportunity for man's worship and for his service. Here is only a child to be amused. . . . To help us grow by keeping our minds and hearts open, is part of the task of the Church.

Umphrey Lee proved himself to be a true Southerner, if an adopted one, in his increasing fear of omniscient federalism. Love of local liberties and awareness of the threat to individual freedom led him to a distrust of national authority. He tried to distinguish between controls which need to be exercised by government and those which should be left to voluntary associations or to the individual. ("A Word About Government Control.") He feared that after World War II, misery abroad and a threat of depression at home might encourage totalitarian trends in the United States. (Report to the Board of Trustees, June 8, 1942.)

In exploring the reasons for the centralization of governmental power, he placed some of the blame on the stream of novels of the 1920's that spread distrust of local government by "depicting the meanness and crudity of small-town life," villages made up of Babbits, of people with frustrated lives, of hyprocrites and charlatans. According to Dr. Lee, the intended political moral of these novels was that one cannot trust government in the hands of the uninformed and unsophisticated in the Bible Belt and in the Middle West; and the only safe course was to remove control as far as possible from the local incompetents. (*Render unto the People,* pp. 50-59.)

Twelve years later, in 1958, in speaking of bribes, gifts, and corruption in government, Dr. Lee wrote:

The whole trouble, as I see it, stems back into the concentration of too much power into too few hands. You can kiss babies and shake hands, but you can't do too much for thousands of voters. But when a bureaucracy system concentrates power into a few hands, you have the seeds of corruption, direct or indirect.

If the power were scattered, the need to see the right people would be diminished. The South Pole explorer many years ago who said that what he missed most during his long stay in the Antarctic was temptation, was speaking a deep truth. If you remove temptation you stop a lot of transgressors. ("As I See It," June 15, 1958.)

The next week, in "As I See It," still commenting on the Sherman Adams case, gifts of mink coats, and deep-freezers to governmental officers, Dr. Lee humorously suggested that the rule should be "no gifts while in office" but, upon leaving office, grateful friends could arrange a shower. (June 22, 1958.)

"As I See It"

As Umphrey Lee saw it, the trend was toward swallowing up individuals, moving toward putting more and more responsibility upon lawmakers and less and less upon the individual citizen. Some nostalgia for less crowded times shows when he noted that in our pioneer communities "neighbors helped as neighbors do not help today." Then the country was large and control from a distance was difficult. A pioneer could preserve what he felt to be his "personal rights and essential freedoms" by heading West. Lee remarked that many agreed with the cowboy song: "I like my fellowman best, when he is scattered some." ("As I See It," January 20, 1957.) He philosophized that our physical frontiers are no longer vast and "there are few places where a man can go without sooner or later finding one of his neighbors passing by in an automobile." He noted that one particular old man did just that by living in an isolated section of the Southwest. When asked how he could endure to live in such a lonely isolation he replied, "Mister, you would be surprised to know how many people I don't like don't live here." ("As I See It," January 20, 1957.)

Yet, Dr. Lee felt that there must be "some middle ground between those who claim government must do nothing for the people and those who would have government do everything. In some fields we have to invoke common action, and offsetting the effects of climate is one of the fields." He elaborated his premise with this folklore:

It is amazing how much human beings can endure, but there is a limit even to the most patient. . . .

A somewhat irreverent summing up of the situation when too much bad luck breaks through an iron reserve is in the story of the farmer who lost his wheat crop. He said: "The Lord giveth and the Lord taketh away." His hogs died of the cholera. The victim repeated: "The Lord giveth and the Lord taketh away." His tractor got out of hand and tore down one side of his barn. He said:

"The Lord giveth and the Lord taketh away." A tornado came along and whisked his house from over his head and left him standing in the big road in his nightshirt in a pouring rain. He said: "Lord, this is getting ridiculous." ("As I See It," May 12, 1957.)

Although Dr. Lee died in 1958 before hippies, alienation, involvement, dialogue, confrontation, pot, grass, relevance, etc. became common words in our vocabulary, he seemed to have sensed the trend that finally erupted in violence and hatred. He did not comment often on the racial problem and, as quoted previously, did not believe in forced segregation or forced integration. ("As I See It," May 4, 1958.) He spoke in terms of simple justice: to preserve the self-respect of those of different races; to give opportunity for education, making a living, to provide the peace and the security that are necessary if people are to be treated as human beings; to give every race its chance to make its contribution to art, science, and citizenship in the world. ("The Chinese and the Race Problem.") There was a plea for generous idealism, cool-headed moderation, a humanistic approach that worked for mediation, for conciliation. On the racial question Dr. Lee was a gradualist and, at the SMU School of Theology, he put this into practice. Yet he understood the frustrations of the disadvantaged and wrote, "It is easy to preach patience when we ourselves are well fed, when we have economic security. We are not geared to patience." (*Render unto the People,* p. 149.)

Dr. Lee recognized the heritage of hatred and violence that has manifested itself many times in our history and identified it as a "clear and present danger" for the future. He quoted Tocqueville of the 1830's: "If ever the free institutions of America are destroyed, that event may be attributed to the omnipotence of the majority, which may at some time urge the minorities to desperation and oblige them to have recourse to physical force. Anarchy will then result, but it will have been brought about by despotism." (*Render unto the People,* p. 41.)

The following excerpt from sermons published in 1925 reveals a mind attuned to current issues:

There is a strange confidence in temporary violence. There is a widespread belief in the religious efficacy of the laying on of violent hands. We are quite ready to convert men by methods which smell of the Inquisition, and we are tolerant of mobs if only they punish guilty men. Woman's suffrage was not achieved by those who poured acid into mail boxes. . . . Extension of the franchise came as a result of years of insistent propaganda, not as the result of a brief flurry of physical violence. I do not think that Carrie Nation did much for prohibition. (*Jesus the Pioneer,* pp. 90-91.)

Thirty-two years later he was writing:

Three times in my life I have been caught—in spite of all my efforts to escape—in mobs. . . . In each instance I was scared, but I came away with a hearty respect for what we call law and order. And in each instance I learned again that mobs destroy. Mobs beheaded the king and queen and the nobility of France, but they also opened the way for Napoleon and dictatorship. In many parts of the world the mob has made dictators possible. ("As I See It," September 29, 1957.)

In 1946 it was difficult to imagine the extent of future racial eruption, but Dr. Lee was speaking then of almost inevitable class war and the necessity to correct social evils using persuasion and not violence. He emphasized that we have a democratic "duty to conform, as well as a duty to dissent." His words have a ring of the 1960's when he wrote: "Even good people, eager to serve justice, are willing to attack the law and the courts and to encourage others to do so. Manifest injustice must be attacked, but to make the laws and the courts the criminals is a poor way to protect the silken cords that bind society together." (*Render unto the People,* p. 160.)

Again in 1956, in the lecture, "Just Before the Battle, Brother," Dr. Lee protested, "Divisions of opinions we must have; rivalries we must have, but hatreds we do not need. Hatreds we cannot afford."

In one of his few references to the theater in his published works, Dr. Lee wrote of the play "Liliom," produced in New York in the early 1920's. He and his youthful contemporaries interpreted the play as a "glorification of rebellion." In speaking of the theme of this play, the revolt of the youth of the 20's, he might be speaking of the rebellion of the 60's:

The students of today inherit the literature of revolt from their fathers and they inherit also a regimented world without parallel in our history—and we are sometimes impatient with them because they are confused! . . . The clamor for revolt in the 20's was, much of it, absurd: there is no such thing as absolute freedom. Some regulation in a complex and growing society is necessary. But we ought to get nearer the problem than the rebels and the defenders of everything that is, usually do. ("As I See It," November 24, 1957. The reference is to the play "Liliom" by Molnar, produced by the Theater Guild in New York.)

But Dr. Lee also often spoke in defense of the younger generation. In 1944, he gave an address in Nacogdoches, Texas, on the subject, "Can Colleges Help Preserve Democracy?" in which he said, "An older man asked whether I think that the younger generation is worse than their fathers. I replied that I should think so if I hadn't known their fathers. My companion added that he would have come to the same conclusion if he had not known their grandfathers." In 1952, at the first all-school convocation of the fall semester at SMU, he mentioned wars, combat service, threat of business depression, adding, "Your generation is no worse than any other. It is only under more suspense." He continued that he was not the sort of educator who believed that a person's character was set, as in cement, by the time he was five years old. Character continues to be molded as persons continue to grow, but "it takes a mighty lot of influence to change your fundamental attitudes after you are seventeen."

From time to time over the years, Dr. Lee warns against idealistic fanaticism as having no place in a democracy—a system which is not a philosophical one as nazism and communism pretended to be but a practical system based on a belief in the individual, individual enterprise and liberty. "We do not need ideological groups with a do-or-die attitude." ("Just Before the Battle, Brother.") He recognized that ideological enmities are implacable and resist settlements that could be reached by compromise and negotiation, and he seemed to anticipate the idealistic cults of a later time. Those who might have been religious martyrs in the days of the Romans now asked to be dragged and beaten as a sacrifice for a social and moral ideal. There is an implication that we would be in difficulty if we rejected practical politics for ideological doctrinaire notions. "When groups are organized to protect or secure what seem vital rights, the picture changes. Dissent takes on the color of heresy." (*Render unto the People,* pp. 53-55 and 128.)

Dr. Lee believed in the effectiveness of our two-party system of government as providing a stability and continuity superior to that of other countries. He illustrated his point with an example from Germany under the Weimar Republic when there were thirty-odd parties. Standing in the Tiergarten in Berlin the day the Reichstag was convened in 1932, he watched some workmen leading a little gray donkey. Someone called out: "Here comes a delegate to the Reichstag! " and another asked, "What party does he represent? " The whole parliamentary system had fallen so low as to forfeit all respect. ("Just Before the Battle, Brother.")

Study of the American character convinced Dr. Lee that we are doubly fortunate not to have adopted the French or English legislative system where governments fall when they cease to command a majority in parliament: "With the American temperament the possibility of ousting a government fifteen days after it took power might be irresistible. Our system is clumsy and slow, but it is remarkable how many burning issues which cry to high heaven for settlement during the second year of a presidential term fade into insignificance before the four years have passed." (*Render unto the People*, p. 46.)

Dr. Lee had much to say about the need for a responsible electorate. Just because a man votes does not necessarily mean that he is well-informed or well-intentioned. He might be like the old man who said, "I haven't made up my mind yet which side I'm on, but when I do I'm going to be bitter about it," or the Methodist steward who voted "No" on the ground that so long as he was a member of the board no proposition should be carried unanimously. ("Can College Help Preserve Democracy?")

There are warnings that what counts is the kind of majority; dictators do not always come as the result of a *coup d'état*. They may be established and supported by a majority.

In later years Dr. Lee might have been dubbed with the political label of conservative, but from him a great deal about genuine liberalism could be learned. Perhaps he was a "liberal-conservative." He had great faith in the largeness of the human spirit and an abiding devotion to democracy. "If democracy will not bring the millennium, neither will any other kind of government" (*Render unto the People*, p. 150); but to bear the attacks of "racial bigotry, arrogance, ambition, and greed" democracy must be supported by a mighty core of religious people, for people who have been educated enough to know their rights but not educated enough to secure them through the democratic process need, also, religious teaching if they are to have the patience that must be a necessary part of democracy. "And those Christians who believe in such worth [man's] that government should be 'of the people, by the people, for the people,' hold this not as self-evident, not on the basis of some theory of history, not as a hypothesis of pragmatic philosophy, but as a corollary of their faith in God. . . . It appears, then, that democracy rests upon the Christian ethic, our enemies themselves being witnesses." ("The Spiritual Basis of Democracy.")

In 1946, Dr. Lee predicted that the mind of the United States and the world was headed toward sensational change. One of the great contests going on was between paganism and Christianity, a battle for the heart and mind of man, and that, if the majority became "convinced that the good things for man, sought by religion, are in the gift of government," then Christianity as he had known it would pass. If this should occur, democracy would be in danger. (*Render unto the People,* p. 64.)

The last war and the atomic bomb had, in Dr. Lee's opinion, elevated the desire for security at the expense of individual freedom and the freedom to criticize. This he considered a threat to religion, since "no church can fulfill its functions, and no individual his religion, unless both are free from restraint by the orthodoxy of either political or economic blocs or by the fanaticism of nationalism. . . . Of all emotions fear is the most favorable to regimentation. . . . To those who are afraid, dissent appears dangerous and heretics become traitors." (*Render unto the People,* p. 54.)

Dr. Lee accepted the idea of a democracy based on majority rule but continued to ask pertinent questions about that majority: its quality; its education; its interest in legislation;

its assumption of responsibility and awareness of ideas versus action, rhetoric versus reality; its resistance to the modern methods and devices of persuasion in mass control through newspapers, radio, television, voice amplification (the bull horn). (*Render unto the People,* pp. 129-57.)

He cautioned: "The government in Washington will rarely be better than the government in the separate states or in the city of Podunk; and the government in Washington will never be more moral than the American home." ("Moral Cleanup Nation's Hope.")

However, it was an optimistic Lee who, on another occasion in a radio address, reminded his audience: "There have been critical times like this before: the Fall of the Roman Empire, the Reformation, the French Revolution. In each of these times there were profound changes. Something old disappeared, something new came to life. . . . One does not have to be foolishly optimistic to realize that people—civilization— survived." ("The Community of the Confident.")

XIV

"A Scholar Who Envisioned Here a Great Independent University"

The last home shared by Umphrey and Mary Lee was at 3307 Southwestern in north Dallas. Dr. Lee bought this property when he resigned from the presidency of Southern Methodist University. The treasures accumulated during thirty-seven years of marriage, particularly during the twelve years in the president's house on Marquette, had to be fitted into the house on Southwestern. The most formidable problem was the disposition of Dr. Lee's books, a scholar's library, and one of the most impressive and extensive private collections in the area. It represented a remarkable financial outlay for a man whose resources had been his stipend as a minister and later his salary as a college dean and university president.

The new home would not hold all the volumes, and a four-way division was finally arrived at. The books needed in Dr. Lee's current literary projects were taken to the carrel in Fondren Library. The walls of the little room were filled from floor to ceiling. Umphrey, Jr., a professor of English, selected and took to his home literary classics and modern fiction associated with his field of work. The shelves in the house on Southwestern absorbed more of the volumes, and the remaining books were placed in storage.

After Dr. Lee's death, Umphrey, Jr. made a further selection of books for his own library, and SMU received some 500 of the Lee collection as a valued gift. Approximately 200 of these books are in the Bridwell Library of the Perkins School

211

of Theology at SMU. Many were published in the seventeenth and eighteenth centuries. Included are two books by Samuel Wesley: *The History of the Old Testament in Verse,* London, 1704, in three volumes; and a huge tome, *Dissertations on the Book of Job,* in Latin, published in London in 1736.

John Wesley quoted much from William Cave's *Primitive Christianity.* There is a copy of this work published in London in 1682. William Dell's *Several Sermons and Discoveries* (1652) and *The Tryal of Spirits, both in Teachers and Hearers* (London, 1693) were referred to as his own books in Dr. Lee's doctoral dissertation. Included in the Bridwell collection are such rare books as a *Call to a Devout and Holy Life* by William Law (1729) and among later books, *The Life of Trust. A Narrative of the Lord's Dealings with George Müller* (1837).

There is an interesting four-volume set of *The Independent Whig,* dated 1743 (first published in 1720). Dr. Lee owned a ten-volume set of *The Ante-Nicene Fathers,* edited by Alexander Roberts and James Donaldson, and a thirteen-volume set of *The Nicene and Post-Nicene Fathers,* edited by Philip Schaff. They are now in the Bridwell reference room.

The 300 books in Fondren Library at SMU further illustrate the extent of the intellectual curiosity of this eclectic man. There are half a dozen books on trout fishing, volumes on philosophy, and many historical tomes. A nine-volume set of the works of Alexander Pope is a reminder of Dr. Lee's two years at the University of Texas and his association with the authority on Pope who introduced the young Lee to serious research. The fascination with the history of Texas and the American West is obvious. There are more than 100 treatises on that area. The range of other subjects is great—from R. C. Armstrong's *Buddhism and Buddhists in Japan* to R. L. Taylor's *W. C. Fields, His Follies and His Fortune;* and from *Shanghai Pierce, A Fair Likeness* by Chris Emmett, to *Seven Years*

Travel in Central America by Julius Froebel (1859), or *The Brave Bulls* by Tom Lea.

The first summer after Dr. Lee became chancellor was spent in Georgetown. In the fall, Dr. and Mrs. Lee were back in Dallas, although Dr. Lee was still following a rest schedule and did not appear at meetings of the executive committee of the board of trustees, of which he was an ex officio member, until March of 1955. After that he attended twenty-five of the thirty-seven meetings of the board of trustees or of the executive committee that were called between then and June 1958.

One of his rare public campus appearances after his illness was at the dedication of the Seismological Station at the University, to thank the Dallas Geophysical Society for their sponsoring of the observatory and to express appreciation to contributors who had furnished most of the funds.

The year 1955 was a more active one for Dr. Lee, and a memorable one. He received many honors, and he participated in the activities surrounding the inauguration of the new president of Southern Methodist University on May 5. In January, President and Mrs. Tate had given a reception honoring Chancellor and Mrs. Lee. The next month the chancellor was honored by being named to the College of Electors of the "Hall of Fame for Great Americans." Other electors were outstanding figures such as Herbert Hoover, Nathan M. Pusey of Harvard, Senator Fulbright, and John Dos Passos, the author. Every five years the electors are asked to vote on the inclusion of prominent Americans to the Hall of Fame on the New York University campus. Dr. Lee cast his first and only ballot in October.

On March 1, 1955, the newly established Faculty Senate at SMU met, elected officers, and began working on plans for effective functioning. This achievement was the culmination of a number of years of investigation and planning, begun during Dr. Lee's presidency. It placed in the hands of the faculty more responsibility for University policy and planning, particularly in nonacademic matters, and set up committees to establish orderly procedures for the operation of certain internal affairs.

The Dallas Rotary Club elected Dr. Lee to honorary membership in recognition of his twenty-five-year association with them which included several years of service on their board. On "Umphrey Lee Day" at Rotary the honoree commented that we need better listeners, for "now we hear more than we can digest," and he facetiously gave four qualifications for successful public speaking:

1 Be against something;
2 Fall into the mood of the times (now optimistic, now pessimistic, now confused);
3 Indicate that there are not many people who know what is really going on;
4 Leave the impression that you are one of the few courageous enough to stand up and tell the truth.

Other speaking engagements began to appear on his calendar again: for the Leadership Conference in Mineral Wells, Texas; at the National Conference of Christians and Jews in San Antonio, Texas; at various organizations in Dallas; and at other universities.

The Lees returned from their summer home in Colorado in time to be guests of honor at a testimonial dinner in the soon-to-be dedicated Umphrey Lee Student Center on September 23, 1955. It was a time for praise and remembering. At age sixty-two Dr. Lee was still surrounded by many friends from college and young ministerial days. One of these, his roommate at Columbia in 1916, was Maurice T. Moore, a prominent New York lawyer, trustee of Columbia University, and public figure, who spoke of meeting Umphrey Lee in 1912, when Moore was a sophomore at Trinity University in

Waxahachie, Texas, and the "tall, gangly, and extraordinary young Umphrey transferred there as a junior. He was already a great speaker, . . . expressed himself with poetic imagination, with humor, and with that inspired economy of language and always to a very simple point or two that you could take away and treasure and chuckle over and never forget."

The two literary societies at Trinity University had vied for Umphrey; the Ratio-Maeonian Society won out over the Philo Sappho Society. Maurice Moore took up debating and he and Umphrey Lee made a winning team, ending a glorious year by defeating the Philo Sapphoes in the grand finale of the spring. Mr. Moore continued:

"That year he persuaded me to go out for what was then called the State Oratorical. There were some eight universities who were represented in the competition. The University of Texas was the colossus and after his own unique intelligence efforts, Umphrey reported that it was the representative of the University of Texas that we had to beat. . . .

"Well I went out for it with my friend Umphrey Lee back of me. With his invaluable help and that of 'Old Livy,' that wonderful Professor Livingston who was our Professor of English, I wrote an oration. I shudder when I think of it today, and I am sure that Umphrey had many qualms.

"And then it came to the day when we were to go to Waco. . . . Now Umphrey was never a man to abandon a project—never a man to abandon a man in need—he was always one to see it through. He went down with me on the old Interurban to Baylor. We went down in the early afternoon and he put me to bed like the good coach and trainer he was.

"And then he called on the other boys, including that boy from the University of Texas, and kept them awake that afternoon. He has always said that little strategy of his was the real clincher. In any event, we won. You see this old turnip watch

—that was the prize, the symbol of our winning—and I have treasured it always.

"Modesty forbids my telling you about the other extra-curricular activities we took part in. Nor will I tell you how we went on to Columbia together. I wish simply to repeat that he had untold influence on me and my life, and if I didn't turn out as well as he hoped, it wasn't his fault."

The Umphrey Lee Student Center was formally dedicated on the afternoon of November 3 with a ceremony participated in by representatives of the board of trustees of Southern Methodist University, of the student body, the Center's student governing board, and the administration. The permanent dedicatory plaque read:

UMPHREY LEE

First President of the Student Body

Fourth President of the University 1939-1954

A scholar who envisioned here a great, independent university. Free under God to seek and transmit knowledge and wisdom. He guided this institution toward that goal.

The portrait of Dr. Lee which hangs in the Umphrey Lee Student Center was a gift of the senior class of 1954. Other memorials to Dr. Lee remain at Southern Methodist University and in Dallas. A life-sized portrait by artist Alexander Clayton was commissioned by Mr. and Mrs. Fred Florence and hangs in the office of the president.

In the center of the SMU Law School quadrangle glows an eight-column white marble cenotaph, The Umphrey Lee Memorial to the Rule of Law. "Through vision, courage and love for his fellowman, Umphrey Lee left an enduring heritage." It was commissioned by the Hoblitzelle Foundation and dedicated in 1959. At the time of his death Dr. Lee was chairman of the board of trustees of the Hoblitzelle Foundation.

In 1960, the Umphrey Lee School (Elementary) on Racine Drive in Dallas was dedicated. Mrs. Umphrey Lee and Mr. and Mrs. Umphrey Lee, Jr. could not come from Louisburg, North Carolina, for the ceremony but, at their request, Dr. Hemphill Hosford presented their gift to the school, a duplicate of a portrait of Dr. Lee which hangs in the Umphrey Lee Student Center at Southern Methodist University.

During his presidency, Dr. Lee initiated moves to expand the University's graduate program. In 1957, President Tate reported to the board of trustees that Chancellor Lee had continued his investigation of the graduate programs of Emory University, Ohio State University, Harvard University, and the Massachusetts Institute of Technology, and that SMU was now ready with a plan to proceed with some programs leading to the Ph.D. degree.

In the years 1956 and 1957, Dr. Lee seemed to be almost back on his old speaking schedule, for he lectured at Southwestern University, Oklahoma City University, Oklahoma A. & M. College, gave the Fondren lectures at SMU, and addressed the ninth World Methodist Conference at Lake Junaluska, North Carolina, speaking on "The Formative Period of American Methodism." In 1956, Abingdon Press brought out *A Short History of Methodism* by Umphrey Lee and William Warren Sweet.

For Christmas 1957, the Lees' Christmas card expressed, in poetic words, Dr. Lee's oft-repeated theme of "joy," "of singing," "of sweet music," "of a joyful noise" from the "other side."

Like John Wesley, he was interested in helping the Christian to live a Christian life in a world as he finds it, to find the joy in Christian life, and to help make today's world a better one to live in. In his sermon "The City to Come" (his sermons were given a title only when they appeared in print) , he said, "We hope and labor for a better earth, and believe in the city not made with hands. We do not seek to visualize or explain, but in this hope we sing." In *Our Fathers and Us,* Dr. Lee points to the songs of joy of the early Methodists—the happy songs of faith in God and life after death. "The Methodists may have been a noisy people, but it was usually intended for a joyful noise" (p. 40) .

In his booklet *For the Rising Generation,* Dr. Lee traces the development of church colleges in the United States and ends, "The story of Methodist education . . . should be set to music, for it is a saga that calls for the sound of trumpets" (p. 29) .

In his last book, *Our Fathers and Us,* these words end the last chapter:

In *Pilgrim's Progress* when Christian had crossed the river and divested himself of his mortal garments he heard the sound of trumpets and when Mr. Valiant-for-truth passed over "all the trumpets sounded for him on the other side."

These are great words, among the greatest in our Christian heritage. But I should like most humbly to suggest that the contribution of the Methodists to a changing world was largely in their belief that they on this side of the dark waters caught the sound of trumpets.

In Dr. Lee's sermons there are many references to these heavenly sounds, the "sound of trumpets," and in the last Christmas card it is "heaven's melodious strains":

> Calm on the listening ear of night
> Come heaven's melodious strains
> Where wild Judea stretches far
> Her silver-mantled plains.
> (Edmund H. Sears.)

Completion of the book *Our Fathers and Us* was the major project of the last year. This book has been described as Dr. Lee's "final bequest to Methodism." In it he maintains that "Methodism is essentially an evangelistic movement and is not a theological system"—a missionary movement which attempted to relate religion to all economic and social classes. It was not a protest movement against the Anglican Church but an attempt to give religious meaning to all classes of men.

When the ordered world of Wesley's childhood began to break up, people were hesitant and afraid both of this world and that other world after death. Methodism's gospel was:

to deliver men and women from the fear of that other world, and thus, to give peace and joy in this world. True, they did not believe that their peace and joy could be had without effort or without trust in God through Jesus Christ.

But they gave to their hearers an invitation to a peaceful and happy life. And if they came to realize how few, like Arvid Gradin, attained to that sweet calm of spirit in this life, still they held to their ideal. And they preached salvation now. (*Our Fathers and Us*, pp. 59-60.)

Almost the last words he wrote rang with hope. In interpreting the nature of the early Methodist message, he spoke of its "note of confidence in an age of dissolution." He further explained that the Methodists were not preoccupied "with the other world but with the duties of man in this world," and they were also concerned with the "ordinance of a living institution, . . . the actual means of grace." Lee then reminded his readers of the Methodists' "emphasis on joy, the singing message of these people . . . at a time when so few people had anything to sing about" (p. 113).

However, if the early Methodists often sang a "happy song," they just as often sang a sad song. Dr. Lee wrote, "Anyone who knows the literature of the mid-eighteenth century knows that it dripped with tears." Emotion was an integral part of the literature of the day, and Lee felt it only "fitting that the religious movement called Methodism should also lay great stress upon the emotions." Gray's "Elegy in a Country Church-yard" might just as well be entitled "A Dirge in a Graveyard" for it reflected an emotional era. "When the Methodists talked about being of a 'sorrowful spirit' they were only talking the language of the eighteenth century. The fear of death was characteristic of the eighteenth century as it was of the Middle Ages" (pp. 32-34).

Umphrey Lee's long involvement with the life and works of John Wesley is understandable, was perhaps inevitable. He was a Wesley-like Christian. He recognized that John Wesley, perhaps intuitively, understood the pressing needs of the eighteenth century and brought the Christian message in words the people could understand. Lee wrote that the jargon of any profession, "familiar enough to its devotees, is too frequently used in an attempt to explain what it means. . . . Wesley had the habit of writing in plain and simple language and speaking in the same way" (pp. 46-47). So did Umphrey Lee.

From time to time over the years, Dr. Lee spoke about death and immortality. In one of his first published sermons he wrote:

This door toward the future is the Christian's way out of sorrow, as it is his way out of narrow living and circumscribed habits of mind. To those whose faith has given life a real meaning, not even death raises brazen walls that shut out all light. Those who live by faith lift up their eyes to a door standing open in heaven, for they have learned

> "The truth to flesh and sense unknown,
> That life is ever Lord of Death,
> And Love can never lose its own."

(*Jesus the Pioneer*, p. 20.)

At Eastertime 1957, in his column "As I See It," Dr. Lee had elaborated on the theme that popular conception of immortality had, traditionally, emphasized youth:

What people think about, if they think at all of another life, is the continuance of the better part of their lives. . . . We may repeat our mistakes but we don't want to take eternity to do it. . . . The weariness and the shock of battle, the burdens of old age, the pain of continued illness: they are not hard to leave. But there are those things which ought not to go out into cold and darkness. (April 21, 1957.)

In the twilight of his life, in his last Easter message, Dr. Lee wrote again of the emphasis upon youth in the conception of immortality:

Easter is rooted in man's longing to overcome Death. . . . On the western portals of the great Medieval cathedrals, Resurrection never shows human beings arising from the tombs as old men and old women. Men and women arise from the graves in youth: Resurrection is the Resurrection of life at its best. ("As I See It," April 6, 1958.)

The spring of 1958 passed quickly and on May 8, a month and a half after his sixty-fifth birthday, the board of trustees of Southern Methodist University met in regular session and named Umphrey Lee, Chancellor Emeritus and Professor of History Emeritus to take effect on June 30, at the end of the current school year. A noon luncheon in the Great Hall of the Umphrey Lee Student Center followed the morning session. A former classmate heading another college, Dr. J. Earl Moreland of Randolph-Macon; Bishop A. Frank Smith of Houston; Mr. Eugene McElvaney, Chairman of the executive committee of the board of trustees; and President Tate who presided, all spoke in praise of Dr. Lee.

The University senate's reception for retiring faculty and staff members was scheduled at 3:30 in the afternoon of Sunday, May 14, in the parlors of Fincher Memorial Building. When four o'clock had passed, but Dr. and Mrs. Lee had not arrived to join the waiting receiving line of honorees, a hurried telephone inquiry was hesitantly made. Dr. Lee answered and replied, apologetically, that they were not going to be able to come. No explanation was forthcoming, but the assumption was that Mary Lee, already depressed, could not bring herself to go through with this sad, final, public ceremony of separation from the institution that had meant so much to Umphrey Lee.

On June 2, in the Southern Methodist Coliseum (now Moody Coliseum), Dr. Lee gave the annual statement to graduates, talking about the "beat generation." He completed the official school year by attending the meeting of the executive committee of the board of trustees on June 6. From then on he was busy at the University getting things in order to vacate his chancellor's office, trying to complete his book, and preparing his next Sunday's newspaper column before he left for his summer in Georgetown.

Sunday evening, June 22, Mrs. Matchett and her daughter, Mrs. Stover, dropped by the house on Southwestern for a little chat with the Lees, as they did frequently. Mary Lee was not in a cheerful mood, but Umphrey Lee was buoyed up by the prospect of completing his writing project and getting started for another lovely summer in Colorado. He was sure that Colorado would restore his wife's health and optimism. When the visitors were ready to leave he went out to the car with them and, as he had done many times, appealed to Mrs. Matchett to encourage Mrs. Lee to get started on her packing and preparations so that they could leave for Georgetown on Thursday.

Monday, the twenty-third of June, was a bright, warm June

day in Dallas. There was a promise of the summer heat, soon to descend on the city, that prompted nostalgic thoughts of the coolness of the Colorado mountains. Dr. Lee was eager to get started but was delaying their departure until Thursday to be present at a Wednesday night dinner honoring longtime associates Wiggs N. Babb and Layton W. Bailey who were also retiring after many years in the business office of the University. Dr. Lee and Dr. Hosford had been consulting about appreciative and humorous remarks they intended to make at the banquet.

In early afternoon Dr. Lee was working in his hidden carrel on the third floor of Fondren Library. As usual he had several projects in process. He had prepared his column "As I See It" for the next Sunday's *Dallas Times Herald*. He had already done a great amount of research for a piece of nineteenth-century American history for a book which he was tentatively calling *The Lower Road*. It dealt with a pioneer road in Texas which was the southern version of the Oregon trail.

He had long been making plans and collecting material for a book which would have moved him into the field of literary criticism. He had carried on an extensive study of American fiction and believed that he could show that the twentieth-century American's religious imagery, his emotional reaction, and theological participation were largely conditioned by the American Novel.

Only recently he had been discussing with another member of "The Thirteen Club," Mr. W. P. Bentley, a member of both the American and English Societies of Psychical Research, the preparation of a book dealing with mystical religious experiences for which Lee had long been collecting material.

At the time of the publication of his works on John Wesley, Dr. Lee had been accused of being a Methodist humanist, of putting secular ideas too much into the study of Wesley and attempting to explain everything in natural terms, playing down emotion and the supernatural. The effort to adapt to twentieth-century ideas runs through much of Dr. Lee's approach to religion. Although skeptical, he had, as he grew older, begun to read some works on parapsychology and collect material on reported mystical experiences in religion.

Mr. Bentley had discussed with him a childhood experience that Dr. Lee remembered and had pondered many times. When Lee was twelve years old his father, Josephus Lee, was seated at his desk writing a letter. Umphrey was asleep on a couch across the room. When Josephus started to address the envelope he could not remember the name of the town. Umphrey, in his sleep, called out distinctly the name his father was attempting to recall.

Perhaps Dr. Lee planned to take some of his files with him to Colorado. Undoubtedly he would be pondering his next project and, as usual, trying out some of his ideas on his friends as he fished or sat with them in his little Victorian living room in Georgetown. But today he was doing his last work on the book to be called *Our Fathers and Us*.

He turned to his telephone and dialed the number of the office of the SMU Press. His voice came through with its usual magic, saying that he had finished, and perhaps they would like to send someone for the manuscript. Within twenty minutes Mrs. Elizabeth Matchett Stover, sales and promotion manager of the Press, had made her way down from the third floor of Perkins Administration Building and across the campus to Fondren Library. She felt the warm glow of anticipation, that the prospect of a few words with Umphrey Lee always evoked, as the elevator took her to the third floor of Fondren Library, and she hurried down the hall to Dr. Lee's small study.

But she was too late. No one in this world would speak with Dr. Lee again. For a few moments she thought that he was just asleep on the couch, and then, stunned, she realized that his stillness was the stillness of death.

The flag on the SMU campus was flown at half-staff from the Monday afternoon of his death through the following Wednesday, when funeral services were held at Highland Park Methodist Church in the Gothic sanctuary Dr. Lee had so lovingly helped design, and the funeral cortege slowly wound its way through the campus of the university with whose existence his life had been so closely entwined for forty-three years.

Floods of telegrams, letters, and messages of sympathy arrived at the Lee home on Southwestern. Memorials and eulogies came from across the country, from national figures, educators, and private citizens, the press, organizations he had assisted, associations he had encouraged, Protestants, Catholics, and Jews. The *New York Herald Tribune* carried a tribute to Dr. Lee the day after his death, and newspapers throughout the Southwest editorialized their praise of him. Why Southern Methodist University had attained such phenomenal growth during his administration may be understood by quoting a small portion of these messages, which were printed in six or seven column spreads in Section I of the *Dallas Morning News* and the *Dallas Times Herald*. The *Dallas Times Herald* expressed the loss which Dallas and Texas felt:

A great and good man is gone.
A community, a state and a nation suffered inestimable loss.

Dr. Lee was one of the most beloved citizens of Texas.
The popularity of Dr. Lee, his skill as an administrator, his charm of personality, his broad tolerance and his hard work were important factors in winning for SMU the goodwill and support, not only of Dallas residents of all faiths, but of public-spirited citizens of all Texas and other states.

Dr. Lee was a brilliant and witty speaker. He was also a forceful writer.

Dr. Willis M. Tate, who succeeded Dr. Lee to the SMU presidency: "This is a great personal loss. Umphrey Lee was not only my good friend but my ideal. . . . More than any other man, he is the symbol of the University."

Bishop A. Frank Smith of Houston: "Dr. Lee's death is an incalculable loss to his church and his nation. . . . He possessed the rare combination of belonging to the intelligentsia and at the same time being perfectly at home in the humblest surroundings. His social qualities were superb."

Gov. Price Daniel: "Dr. Lee was one of the state's finest educators and I am grieved to learn of his death."

Senator Ralph Yarborough: "The death of Umphrey Lee is a shock and a loss to everyone who believes in education for free minds. The state has lost not only a great religious leader and a great educator: it has lost more—a balance wheel and a stabilizer against the postwar-waves of hysteria which have swept over our nation and state. Dr. Lee set a tone at SMU; a tone of tolerance, of intellectual freedom that will be sorely missed in Texas. His passing leaves a void in Texas life."

Eugene McElvaney, Chairman of the Executive Committee of SMU's Board of Trustees: "The imprint of his personality and all the elements of greatness it so fully characterized will be deeply and everlastingly imbedded in the history of SMU."

W. W. Caruth, Jr., civic and business leader: "We have seen SMU develop from entirely a local institution to one of the outstanding universities of the nation under his direction."

Hastings Harrison, vice president of the National Conference of Christians and Jews: "He was one of the founders of the National Conference of Christians and Jews in Dallas and I have never known a man who abhorred bigotry and intolerance more than he. Protestants, Catholics and Jews alike share in the great sorrow that has been occasioned by his death."

Tom Unis, city councilman and Catholic Chairman for the NC-CJ: "Dr. Lee's contribution to the spiritual, educational and cultural life of Dallas and the Southwest will serve as a continuing monument to the life of a truly great citizen."

"A Scholar Who Envisioned Here . . ."

Dean Robert G. Storey of the SMU School of Law: "My most recent association with him was his willingness to accept membership on the newly-created Civil Rights Advisory Committee of Texas. He entered into these duties and attended its first meeting with a keen insight and genuine understanding of the importance and difficulty of the problem facing the committee."

Dr. Levi A. Olan, Rabbi of Temple Emanu-El: "His was a distinguished career in religion, education, and citizenship. His faith was universal and enveloped humanity. I feel the sadness of the loss of a dear and faithful friend."

The most touching eulogy of all came from a student in the institution Dr. Lee had loved and given so much of his efforts, affection, and loyalty. This tribute, written by a young man who had never met Dr. Lee, appeared in the editorial column of *The Campus:*

The small room on the third floor of Fondren Library was in the disunited confusion which denoted that work, the work of a scholar and a writer, was its function.

Here it was that Dr. Umphrey Lee spent his time and his energy. This was his hide-away and he loved this room. He died there.

Although we did not know him personally, he had retired from the presidency into the comparatively non-publicized position of Chancellor before we entered school, we could see in this room the manifestation of his personality.

It was a warm room. The walls were obliterated on three sides (except for one window) by shelves upon shelves of books which tilted in no particular direction.

The desk was in mass disarray; papers, folders and books lying in such a way that only Dr. Lee could himself have found what he wanted. His keys were on top of a pamphlet on the University senate. The phone was standing on a book on religion.

There was nothing formal in the room, just as Dr. Lee was not a formal person. He was a warm man, both to his friends and to those whom he did not know so well. His room was warm too, even to a casual observer like ourselves. His intense scholarship and interest in religion and in education could be easily seen by the books in the room.

We students owe the kind of education we receive here today to Umphrey Lee.

This is a man whose personality and interest in academic excellence transformed SMU from a small college into a fine university which will continue to build upon the heritage which he leaves with us.[1]

---

[1] *The Campus,* Jay Brown, editor, June 28, 1958.

Bibliography

Acheson, Sam. "Dallas Pastor's Biography of Founder of Methodism Quotes Valuable New Source Material," *Dallas Morning News,* July 29, 1928.

Beaty, John O. *The Iron Curtain over America.* Dallas, Texas: Wilkinson Publishing Company, 1951.

Bell, B. L. Review of *The Lord's Horseman: John Wesley, The Saturday Review of Literature,* January 26, 1929.

Bradley, Preston. Review of *The Historic Church and Modern Pacifism. Book Week.* March 14, 1943.

Brown, Jay, ed. Editorial on the Death of Dr. Lee. *SMU Campus,* June 28, 1958.

Calhoun, R. L. Review of *The Lord's Horseman: John Wesley, Yale Review,* Autumn, 1929.

Crume, Paul. "SMU Honors First Student President, Now Head of School," *Dallas Morning News,* November 6, 1939.

Cuninggim, Merrimon. "Memorandum on the Negro Problem." (Manuscript)

Dallas Journal. Dallas, Texas. January 26, 1933.

Dallas Morning News. Dallas, Texas. 1929-1958.

Dallas Times Herald. Dallas, Texas. 1939-1958.

Ferguson, W. Review of *The Lord's Horseman: John Wesley. The Bookman,* January 1929.

Fort Worth Star Telegram. November 5, 1939.

Holmes, J. H. Review of *John Wesley and Modern Religion, Books.* October 4, 1936.

Hudson, W. S. Review of *The Historic Church and Modern Pacifism. Journal of Religion,* July, 1943.

Johnson, Doris Miller. *Golden Prologue to the Future: A History of Highland Park Methodist Church.* Nashville, Tennessee: Parthenon Press, 1966.

Johnson, Paul. "A Birthday Letter," *New Statesman,* London, 1969.

Joy, James R. "Book Reviews," *Religion in Life,* Winter, 1937.

Kirby, John L. *Minutes of the Annual Conference of the Methodist Episcopal Church South for the years 1906-1909,* ed. John L. Kirby. Nashville: Smith and Lamar, 1909.

Lee, Josephus. Documents in SMU Archives.

Mason, Alpheus Thomas. *Brandeis.* New York: Viking Press, 1956.

Mayes, Will H. *The Houston Post,* May 28, 1939.

Maxwell, Allen. "Activities of the S.M.U. Press in Relation to John O. Beaty." April 5, 1954. (Manuscript)

Monk, Robert C. *John Wesley and His Puritan Heritage.* Nashville, Tennessee: Abingdon Press, 1966.

Montgomery, D. B. *General Baptist History.* Evansville, Indiana: Courier Company, 1882.

Mood, R. G., ed. *Journal of the North Texas Annual Conference of the Methodist Church South,* 1933.

Nail, Olin W., ed. *The History of Texas Methodism.* Austin, Texas: Capital Printing Company, 1961.

————, ed. *Texas Methodist Centennial Yearbook.* Elgin, Texas, 1935.

The New York Times, December 4, 1944 and January 21, 1945.

Porter, A. D., and Winfield, G. F., eds. *Central Texas Annual Conference, 1917, Methodist Episcopal Church South.* Georgetown, Texas, 1917.

Rucker, Samuel J., ed. *Journal of the Central Texas Conference.* Hillsboro, Texas, 1914.

San Angelo (Texas) Standard. November 2, 1939.

Simpson, J. Fisher, ed. *Journal of the Sixty-Eighth Annual Session of the West Texas Conference: Methodist Episcopal Church, South.* Austin, Texas, 1926.

SMU Campus. 1916 to 1958.

SMU Times. 1915 (later *SMU Campus*).

"SMU Today." (Pamphlet) Dallas, Texas; Winter 1969-70.

Sweet, W. W. Review of *John Wesley and Modern Religion, The Christian Century,* September 9, 1936.

Texas Christian Advocate, April 29, 1926 (Death of Josephus Lee).

Time Magazine, March 5, 1952.

Bibliography

Tolbert, Frank X. "Headliner Portrait." *Dallas Morning News,* June 5, 1949.

"Umphrey Lee Named Chancellor Emeritus." *The Mustang*. Dallas, Texas: SMU Press, May-June 1958.

Vernon, Walter N. *Methodism Moves Across North Texas*. Dallas, Texas: The Historical Society, North Texas Conference, The Methodist Church, 1967.

White, James F. *Architecture at S.M.U.* SMU Press, Dallas, 1966.

Works of Umphrey Lee

Books

The Bible and Business. New York: Richard R. Smith, 1930.

The Historical Backgrounds of Early Methodist Enthusiasm. New York: Columbia University Press, 1931.

The Historic Church and Modern Pacifism. Nashville, Tennessee: Abingdon-Cokesbury Press, 1943.

Jesus the Pioneer and Other Sermons. Nashville, Tennessee: Cokesbury Press, 1925.

John Wesley and Modern Religion. Nashville, Tennessee: Cokesbury Press, 1936.

The Life of Christ: A Brief Outline for Students. Nashville, Tennessee: Cokesbury Press, 1929.

The Lord's Horseman: John Wesley. New York: The Century Company, 1928.

Our Fathers and Us. Dallas, Texas: SMU Press, 1958.

Render unto the People: The Cole Lectures, 1946, Vanderbilt University. Nashville, Tennessee: Abingdon-Cokesbury Press, 1947.

A Short History of Methodism (with Sweet, William Warren). Nashville, Tennessee: Abingdon Press, 1956.

Miscellaneous

"A Report on the Ivory Tower." *Association of American Colleges Bulletin,* March 1953.

"A Word About Government Control." *Dallas Times Herald,* March 19, 1944.

"America. Lewis Timothy, Charlestown. The Printer of Wesley's First Hymn Book, 1737." *Proceedings of the Wesley Historical*

231

Society, December 1921. (Burnley: Printed by Ashworth Nuttall, Bank Parade.)

"As I See It," *Dallas Times Herald.* (A weekly column appearing from September 9, 1956 until July 6, 1958.)

"The Clouds Return After the Rain." (Manuscript.)

"The Community of the Confident." *An Informed Church and Other Messages from the Methodist Hour.* Edited by James W. Sells. Atlanta, Georgia: The Methodist Church, 1947.

"Can Colleges Help Preserve Democracy?" (Manuscript)

"The Chinese and the Race Problem." *Dallas Times Herald,* October 17, 1943.

Directory of Highland Park Methodist Church South.

"Dedication Sermon," *Dallas Morning News,* March 28, 1943.

"The Fondren Lectures." 1956. (On Tape) Bridwell Library, SMU.

"For the Rising Generation." (Booklet) Nashville, Tennessee: The Methodist Publishing House, 1958.

"Freedom from Rigid Creed," *Methodism.* Edited by William K. Anderson. Nashville, Tennessee: The Methodist Publishing House, 1947.

"Institutions of Higher Learning." *Journal of the Uniting Conference of the Methodist Episcopal Church, Methodist Episcopal Church South, Methodist Protestant Church.* Edited by Lud H. Estes and others. Nashville, Tennessee: The Methodist Publishing House, 1939.

"Inaugural Address." *Proceedings of the Inauguration of Umphrey Lee as the Fourth President of Southern Methodist University.* Dallas, Texas: SMU Press, 1939.

"Human Relations and Our Heritage." *Proceedings, Fourteenth Conference: Texas Personnel and Management Association,* 1952.

"History and the Intellectual Climate." *Integration of the Humanities and the Social Sciences: A Symposium.* Edited by Ernest E. Leisy. Dallas, Texas: SMU Press, 1948.

"Higher Education in United Methodism," *The Southwestern Advocate,* March 28, 1940.

"Just Before the Battle, Brother." Lecture to the Dallas Salesmanship Club, 1956. (Manuscript)

Bibliography

"John Wesley's Love Affairs." *The Methodist Quarterly Review,* July 1925.

Letters to Miss Mary C. Sweet. Nine letters written between 1912 and 1916. (SMU Archives)

"The Liberal Arts College Today." (Address delivered December 2, 1940 to the SMU Chapter of the American Association of University Professors. (Typewritten)

Preface to *Medicine for a Sick World* by David Lefkowitz. Dallas, Texas: SMU Press, 1952.

"Moral Cleanup Nation's Hope." Speech delivered at the annual dinner of the Chamber of Commerce of the United States. Printed in the *Dallas Morning News,* August 16, 1951.

"Methodism's Institutions of Higher Learning." *The Southwestern Advocate.* Dallas, Texas, July 20, 1939.

"Our Educational Confusions," *The Mustang.* Dallas, Texas: SMU Press, May 1954.

"The Preacher and the Modern Mind." *School of Religion Notes: The School of Religion of Vanderbilt University.* November 15, 1938. Nashville, Tennessee.

Review of *John Wesley* by Bishop Francis J. McConnell, *Religion in Life:* Autumn, 1939.

"Saints Wanted," *The Southwestern Christian Advocate,* February 28, 1935.

"Shall We Cease Bombing Germany?" *Dallas Times Herald,* March 26, 1944.

"SMU—Present and Future." *The Southwestern Advocate,* Dallas, Texas, February 26, 1942.

"The Spiritual Basis of Democracy." *Christian Basis of World Order: The Merrick Lectures of 1943.* Nashville, Tennessee: Abingdon-Cokesbury Press, 1943.

"To Preserve Freedom, Put Freedom First." Washington, D.C.: Chamber of Commerce of the United States, 1951. (Booklet)

"These Bulwark Free Enterprise." Excerpt from the speech to the National Chamber of Commerce, 1951. Printed in the *Dallas Morning News,* August 14, 1951.

"War Memorial Service Honoring Former Students of the Uni-

233

versity Who Gave Their Lives in World War II." Pamphlet, December 7, 1946.

"Who Liveth and Reigneth." *The Christian Advocate,* March 18, 1942.

"Dedicatory Address." Program for the unveiling and dedication of the monument commemorating the life and service of George Bannerman Dealey. November 14, 1949. Dallas, Texas.

Introduction to *That's All for Today: Selected Writings of Tom Gooch,* edited by Decherd Turner. Dallas, Texas, SMU Press, 1955.

"Thanksgiving 1955" (editorial). *Christianity and Crisis,* November 14, 1955.

Interviews and Letters

Abernathy, Elizabeth (Mrs. B. H.), Registrar of the School of Religion, Vanderbilt University, Nashville, Tennessee. (Retired)

Baker, Dr. George C., Perkins School of Theology, SMU, Dallas, Texas.

Baker, W. Harrison, pastor, Methodist Church, Greenville, Texas.

Bailey, Layton W., Business Manager of SMU. (Retired)

Beaty, Mrs. Tom. Niece of Miss Mary Sweet.

Bentley, W. P., President, Uvalde Construction Company, Dallas. (Retired)

Branscomb, Dr. Harvie, Chancellor of Vanderbilt University. (Retired)

Cuninggim, Dr. Merrimon, President, Danforth Foundation.

Davis, Miss Phoebe A., Secretary of the University, SMU.

Dewitt, Roscoe P. (Dewitt and Lemmon, Architects) Dallas, Texas.

Gambrell, Dr. Herbert. Chairman, Department of History, SMU. (Retired)

Golden, Mrs. J. Roscoe. Former choir director, Highland Park Methodist Church. Member of Music faculty, SMU. (Retired)

Harrison, Hastings. Consultant to the President, SMU.

Hawkins, Loretta (Mrs. Dallas E.), Assistant to the President, SMU. (Retired)

Hay, S. J., Jr., Chairman of the Board, Great National Life Insurance Company, Dallas. (Retired)

Bibliography

Hosford, Dr. Hemphill, Vice President and Provost, SMU. (Retired)

Jordan, Lester, Assistant Athletic Director, SMU. (Retired)

Kenney, Mrs. Edith S., former secretary to Dr. Lee at SMU.

McElvaney, Eugene, Senior Vice President, First National Bank, Dallas, Texas. (Retired)

Martin, Bishop Paul E., Perkins School of Theology, SMU.

Moore, Maurice T. (Law firm of Cravath, Swaine and Moore, New York)

Mouzon, Dr. Edwin D., Jr., Chairman of the Department of Mathematics, SMU. (Retired)

Patterson, Stanley. Superintendent of Buildings and Grounds, SMU. (Retired)

Platter, Paul W., Dallas businessman. (Retired)

Shugart, Mrs. C. O. (Formerly Miss Margaret Todd, secretary to Dr. Lee at Highland Park Methodist Church, Dallas, Texas)

Smith, Dr. Arthur A., Senior vice president and economist, First National Bank, Dallas, Texas (Retired)

Smith, Dr. Richard M., family physician of the Lees. Dallas, Texas.

Starr, Mrs. David. Former secretary to provost Hemphill Hosford, SMU.

Stewart, James H., Consultant to the President, SMU.

Story, Frank J., Highland Park High School, Dallas, Texas. (Retired)

Stover, Mrs. Elizabeth Matchett, Sales and Promotion Manager of the SMU Press. (Retired)

Tate, Dr. Willis M., President, SMU.

Teague, Mrs. Grace N., Librarian of the Kesler Circulating Library, Nashville, Tennessee.

Turner, Decherd H., Librarian of the Bridwell Library, Perkins School of Theology, SMU.

Vernon, Walter N., Administrative Associate and Executive Editor of General Publications, Division of Curriculum Resources, General Board of Education, The United Methodist Church.

Warnick, Mrs. John, Librarian of the Wesley Collection, Bridwell Library, SMU.

Index

Index

Todd, Margaret (Mrs. C. O. Shugart), 74
Tolbert, Frank X., 73, 82, 101
Town and Gown Club, 130
Trinity University, 25-27, 32-35, 58, 214-16
Turner, Decherd H., 88
Twitty, Bryce, 93

Unis, Tom, 226

Vanderbilt University, 46, 80, 82-90, 93-95, 117, 122, 136, 167
Vernon, Walter N., 23, 42, 46, 76, 162, 176

Ward, W. W., 184
Waxahachie, Texas, 25-26, 215
Wesley Bible Chair, 38, 75

Wesley, Charles, 38, 39
Wesley, John, 38-39, 43, 56-58, 60-66, 76-80, 105-7, 122, 130, 160, 167, 212, 217, 219, 220, 223
Wesley Mrs. Molly Vazeille, 62
Wesley, Samuel, 39, 60, 80, 212
Wesley, Mrs. Susanna Annesley, 60
Whaling, Horace M., 66, 91
Whitehurst, John, 26, 27
Whitehurst, John, Jr., 30, 33-34
Willkie, Wendell L., 102, 112
Willson, James, 184
Wilson, Woodrow, 35
Wriston, Henry, 181

Yarborough, Ralph, 226

Zephyr, Texas, 24